INTRODUCTION TO RESEARCH METHODS IN SOCIAL SCIENCES

INTRODUCTION TO RESEARCH METHODS IN SOCIAL SCIENCES

Dr. K. Ravichandran
Dr. S. Nakkiran

ABHIJEET PUBLICATIONS
DELHI 110094

ABHIJEET PUBLICATIONS
2/46 Tukhmeerpur Extension
Delhi-110 094
Phone: 011-22960492, 65698474
E-mail: abhijeetpublication@gmail.com

INTRODUCTION TO RESEARCH METHODS IN SOCIAL SCIENCES

First Published 2009

ISBN 978-81-89886-94-3

PRINTED IN INDIA

Published by J.K. Singh for Abhijeet Publications, Delhi-110 094, Lasertypeset by Gaurav Graphics, New Delhi and Printed at Himanshu Printers, Delhi.

Preface

The objective of social science research is to find solution to the problems of human society. It is concerned with the study of human society, human organizations, and human behaviour. Such problems are broader in nature and fall in the domain of disciplines like Psychology, Sociology, Education, Administration, Management, Commerce, Cooperation, etc. The importance of social research as an instrument of development has been increasing especially in the countries like India. The planned economic growth of the country has opened a large vista of research in social science. This is an oppourtunity as well as a challenge.

We, the authors, feel happy to bring this piece of academic work to the readers. The present work is based on an earlier publication 'An Introduction to Research Methods in Social Sciences' edited by (late) Dr. C.C. Pattanshetty. As lots of changes have taken place since the publication of the previous works, a need to modify the book was felt. We got enough feedback from young researchers doing M.Phil. and Ph.D. Programmes for modifications. The original version of this book had undergone many modifications and additions based on the syllabus prescribed for Research

Methodology for various courses in universities and colleges in southern India. The primary objective of this academic work is to guide the young researchers to understand the basics of social science research and help them to carryout research work.

In this context, we thank the authorities of Gandhigram Rural University, for their encouragements to bring this publication. The encouragements we receive from Dr. B. Subburaj, Professor and Head, Dr. P. Sivaprakasam, Professor and other faculty members in the Department of Cooperation, Gandhigram Rural University needs special mention here. We also extend our sincere thanks to the authorities of Ambo College, Ethiopia for their encouragements for our academic endeavours.

We remember here the esteemed teachers Dr. O.R. Krishnasami and Dr. M.O. Mathew in this context.

K. Ravichandran &
S. Nakkiran

Contents

SECTION – I

MEANING AND DEFINITION OF RESEARCH

1

Meaning and Definition of Research

Human civilization has grown from stage to stage and now has reached a stage where one can enjoy the fruits of scientific advancement and material welfare. Such results are the outcome of new findings, efforts and hard work of a few people. In the absence of such deep enquiries many of our problems might not have been solved. Still we have to solve many problems and researchers are striving hard to find solutions. Hence, research has become a part of our life and continued to co-exist with our civilization.

In the modern complex world, man is faced with many problems; and he alone is responsible for their solution. Problem solving is a technical process which not only requires ingenuity but also a fund of accumulated knowledge and wisdom. Accumulation of new knowledge is essential for humanity's survival and progress and research provides the means for achieving such knowledge. But, mere accumulation of knowledge will be of little use unless it is organized and systematized for broader generalization and for identifying the patterns and laws of human behaviour. Thus, research is a systematic effort at gathering, analysis and interpretation of the problems confronted by humanity. In other words it is a thinking process and a scientific method which is defined by Rummel as, "The systematic and refined use of specialized tools and procedures to obtain a more adequate solution to a problem than would be possible by less discriminatory means. While it is possible to employ scientific method without research, it is not possible to do research without employing scientific method. Hence, research is a scientific system. Research is considered to be the more formal, systematic, intensive process of carrying on the scientific method of analysis. It involves a more systematic structure of investigation usually resulting in some sort of a formal record of procedures and a report of results or conclusions.

Research is not the exclusive preserve of a chosen few. Any individual belonging to any field of activity can undertake research. Intensive study, deep analysis and reflective thinking are the basic ingredients of research. Application of scientific tools and accepted steps and procedure are essential for an ideal research. It must have utility to the society; result in new findings and, or truth must be brought out. Best, views that, "its importance is attested by the tremendous amount of time, manpower and sums of money spent on research by industry, universities and Government". The secret of our cultural development has been research, pushing back the areas of ignorance by discovering new truths which, in turn, lead to better ways of doing things and new and better products.

Need for Research

As the human society is expanding in terms of its material wealth, problems associated with such expansion also develop in various fields. To study such problems of varied nature and find solutions to such problems, research serves as an essential aid. It is the only scientific way of analyzing a problem. Besides, research is essential for the researcher to acquire and familiarize himself with various tools of research. Research tools and techniques are also refined from time to time. It is the duty of a researcher to keep himself abreast with the latest development in his field of research. As evaluation is one of the important aspects of private or public sector projects, research will have immense value to evaluate the failure or success of a project or a programme. Based on such evaluation the project can be aligned in a right direction. Hence, research has occupied a rightful place in all Government departments, industrial concerns and business organization. A majority of the organisations have started separate department called 'Research and Development Wing' to evaluate the programmes, to find solution to problems and to make new discoveries. Research encourages inter-disciplinary approaches in the process. As environment is changing, problems get more complicated. They are not merely discipline-based. Research, problem solving method as it is, should aim at mounting a multi-pronged attack on the different facets of the problem. The inter-disciplinary approach provides a common forum for researchers engaged in diverse fields to coordinate their activities. Research, it should be noted, is a basic ingredient for development and therefore serves as a means for rapid economic development.

Definitions of Research

We have given below some of the generally accepted definitions of research by well-known authors:

Encyclopedia of Social Science: "It is the manipulation of things, concepts or symbols for the purpose of generalizing and to extend, correct or verify knowledge, whether that knowledge aids in the construction of a theory or in practice of an art."

Francis Rummel: "Research is a careful inquiry or examination to discover new information or relationships and to expand and to verify existing knowledge."

M.H. Gopal: "It is essentially a systematic enquiry seeking facts through objective verifiable methods in order to discover the relationship among them and to deduce some broad principles or laws." From the above definitions we can simplify the meaning of research as detailed below:

1. *It is an enquiry or examination seeking facts*

   To find out the truth a researcher can spend any number of years and may come out with the truth through his findings. Such enquiry or examination must be conducted deeply. No shallow enquiry can be called research. Such deep enquiry must probe deep into the problem. Why? How? When? are some of the questions the researcher must pose to himself in the course of his research?

2. *Research aims at finding new truth or knowledge and/or it can confirm the established truth or knowledge*

   When problems occur daily in our life, they provide inspiration to find out new truth. Even the established truths or knowledge or theories can be proved or disproved by research. A truth which was relevant in 18th century may not be relevant to the happenings of today. Hence, it can be disproved.

3. *The purpose of research is to find out solutions to problems*

   If a researcher does not come out with any solution to the problem under enquiry, it is not research: it is "Pseudo research".

4. *Research involves use of accepted scientific tools and statistical methods*

   Before a researcher engages himself in the task of research, he must acquire a fair knowledge of the methods and techniques of research.

Characteristics of Research

Research being a fact finding inquiry, has certain characteristics of its own. It involves scientific procedures and techniques. As social problems can be studied from various angles, the social research should not depend on a single tool or method of research. *Young* observes, "research studies generally utilize not only a variety of techniques but approach the subject matter from a variety of view points. This procedure rests on the assumption that no one point of view or scientific discipline can encompass total social reality. Neither should a single technique of study be regarded as sovereign. Each is a complement to other."

The following are some of the characteristics of research as pointed out by John Best:

1. Research gathers new knowledge or data from primary or first hand sources. It is not research when one merely relates or reorganizes what is already known or what has been written. Research places emphasis upon the discovery of general principles.
2. Research is expert, systematic and accurate investigation. There is no place for approximations and ambiguities in research.
3. Research is logical and objective, applying every possible test to verify the data collected and the procedures employed. The researcher constantly strives to eliminate personal feeling and preference.
4. Research endeavors to gather original data in quantitative terms if possible and to express them as numerical measures. Research is patient and unhurried. The research is willing to exert painstaking effort, suspending judgment to permit the data and logic to lead to a sound conclusion. He realizes that significant findings do not come as a result of hurried and careless procedures.
5. Research requires courage. The researcher should be willing to follow his procedures that may be unpopular and bring social disapproval.
6. Research is carefully recorded and reported. Every term is carefully defined, all procedures are described in detail, all limiting factors are recognized, all references are carefully documented and all results are objectively recorded. "Conclusions and generalizations are cautiously arrived at, with due consideration for all of the limitations of methodology, data collected, and errors of human interpretation."

Social Science Research

The following are some of the accepted definitions of Social Science Research.

Pauline Young: "Social Science Research is a systematic method of exploring, analyzing and conceptualizing social life in order to expand, correct or verify knowledge whether that knowledge aids in the construction of theory or in the practice of an art."

Rummel: "It is devoted to a study of mankind in his social environment and is concerned with improving his understanding of social orders, groups, institutions and ethics."

M.H. Gopal: "It is the scientific analysis of the nature and trends of social phenomena of group or in general, of human behaviour so as to formulate broad principles and scientific concepts."

From the above accepted definitions the following characteristics of social research can be derived:

1. *Social Research is the study of man's behaviour towards the society, hè lives.*

   It encompasses the study of social phenomena covering the economic, political, educational, administrative and related aspects of social life, as also the social groups and institution.

2. *Social research aims at discovery of new facts.*

   The Scientific research techniques are applied to find out truth regarding relationships of various kinds of human behaviour. As *P.V. Young* aptly puts it, "Research is devoted to discover new facts or verify old facts."

3. *Social research assists in the understanding of evolution of new theories.*

   Every research highlights some broad principles, establishes some scientific truths and analyses their sequences, inter-relationship and causal explanations. This results in expansion of knowledge, improvement in the understanding of social phenomena and in the evolution of new theories.

4. *Social research involves the use of scientific methodology.*

   "Research also implies the development of new scientific tools, concepts and theories which would facilitate reliable and valid study of human behaviour."

Social research is a process which goes through all these stages of research from sensing a problem till finding solutions and applying them, which are the ingredients of research. Yet it has certain unique methods and logical problems. In social surveys human beings are the sources of data. The attitudes of respondents and their environment, and honesty, personal values and biases of the researcher, will alter research decision considerably.

Type of Social Research

The Social Research may be broadly classified into following three categories:

1. *Studies which aim at discovery of facts.* Such fact finding studies aim at an accurate assessment of the conditions prevailing. They are based on the empirically gathered primary data.
2. *Studies which aim at interpreting the already available information.* They are based on the secondary data. Such studies are more concerned with the scientific interpretation of the data than merely content with presenting the data.
3. *Theoretical type of research. Such researches are also called pure research.* They neither depend on primary data nor on secondary data. They make contributions to the realm of the theory and add to the existing literature on the subject by way of new interpretation or a different approach to the problem.

Importance of Social Research

The overall objective of any social research is to find solution to the problems of human society. Naturally, social research is concerned with the study of human society, human organizations and human behaviour. Such problems are broader in nature and fall in the domain of disciplines like Psychology, Sociology, Education, Administration, Commerce etc. The importance of social research as instrument of development has been increasing. There has been a significant shift in the emphasis on social research due to the following reasons:

1. The desire to bring about more precision in social research methods and techniques, so as to make them more amenable for better scientific treatment and statistical analysis.
2. Greater emphasis has been placed on improving the quality of research in its different facets—practical, theoretical and methodological. Such improvement is inevitable to make the research conform to the complex social reality.
3. The need for depth and clarity of the study of social phenomena enhances the role of research as a method of seeking explanations to the unexplained social phenomena.
4. Research has a greater role in proving solutions to immediate problems faced by the community.
5. Research not only helps to evolve new techniques and methods but also standardizes them. Such standardized techniques are capable of reproduction.
6. Social research also aids in formulating normative standards which are useful in framing socio-economic plans, for comparison and for evaluation of such plans.
7. Research makes contributions for the expansion of knowledge horizon, as available knowledge on socio-economic conditions, problems and institutions are very limited.
8. The policy and programme oriented research supports the planners and administrators and aids decision making.

The relevance of social research is far greater in developing countries like India which are confronted with complex socio-economic problems like poverty and unemployment. Besides, the peculiar social situations and the existence of innumerable social institutions make the socio-economic matrix a complex one. On the other hand there is no concomitant development in the research techniques and training facilities. In short, in developing countries like India, the researchers find not only opportunities but greater challenges as well. The planned economic growth of the country has opened a large vista of research in social science in India. This is an opportunity as well as a challenge.

Curiosity about the unknown has been the guiding line for humanity and new developments in the fields of science and technology are taking place aided by curiosity. Research which has been playing a pivotal role in the scientific world has occupied a strategic place in social science research also. Research is much more used as a fact finding machinery in social science than as a problem solving device. This has come to be established in developing countries like ours. Research in social sciences has immense value to humanity if it is understood properly and undertaken in the right perspective. Precedents must be created in developing countries in using social research as a problem solving device. This has been aptly pointed out by *S.C. Dube* as follows: "In India, whose ways of life and thoughts are changing very fast, we require a large number of community studies, both in rural and urban areas in the different cultural regions of the country. We owe it to posterity that we leave careful records of contemporary life and cultures. As it is, for their historical and cultural interest above such studies are worth undertaking. But their importance is greater at the present juncture because the country is undergoing significant technological changes and it is necessary for us to assess and evaluate their human implications. Here we have the unique opportunity of masking a 'pre-clinical' study of the communities as they are today and then of studying them stage by stage under the impact of new technological factors. The social scientist can in the first instance, make a really valuable contribution to social planning by publishing full and objective reports of his research; and as the volume of such data grow, ground will be prepared for competent analysis of many problems of deeper theoretical interest. At the present time intensification of community research is an urgent desideratum. As far as possible, in each cultural area it would be desirable to study one or more villages, a representative small town, two or three individual castes within the total network of inter-caste relations; and these studies could then be followed by more intensive investigations into specific problems, such as those of family and kinship, leadership and exercise of authority, social stratification, social change and personality. Preliminary studies can at best offer tentative hypotheses, but for theoretical development of lasting significance we shall have to await more data gathered according to modern techniques of field research.

2

Concepts and Theory

Concepts

Concepts are expressions, which a researcher may use very often in research studies. *Pauline Young* defines it as, "each new class of data isolated from the other classes on the basis of definite characteristics is given, a label—in short—a concept. A concept is in reality a definition in short hand of a class or group of facts." Concepts are to be defined properly as they may have different levels of meaning. When a social researcher uses sampling, the coverage of concepts may vary depending upon the size of samples. A small farmer's size of landholding may vary in an apple growing village of Kashmir to that of a small farmer growing dry crops in Karnataka.

Social science researchers view that mere dictionary definition of concepts is not useful or it will not serve the purpose. Young points out that, "it was realised that dictionary definitions do not suffice for scientific studies". So the researcher has to give, "working definition" or "operational definition". This means a definition of a concept has to suit the researcher's need and environment. As many concepts are not clear or controversial, sometimes, it is difficult to find out terms or concepts which express uniform meaning. Another aspect is the contradiction in the meaning of concepts by various researchers and their basis of scientific exposition. This *Young*, points out as; "as fundamental as the use of precisely defined concepts is to scientific procedure. The development of scientifically defined terminology has been slow and controversial."

Formation of a Concept

For experienced researchers and social scientists it is easy to form concepts, because they come across new observations and new phenomenon. They can very easily name such new set of activity. Another way of forming a concept is by means of continued observation. New observations or new happenings may lead to new behaviour and such things are to be named.

Uses of Concepts

The uses of concepts are manifold:

1. Problem of research can be expressed
2. Avoids repetition and over explanations
3. To frame the objectives
4. To frame hypothesis
5. To find out relationship between variables.

Theory

A theory is set of propositions which can be tested. In other words it 'is a coherent set of hypotheses'. When a set of hypotheses is accepted after testing its truthfulness, the next stage of its growth is theory. A theory is again to be proved or disproved.

Pauline Young defined the nature of a theory as, "it is the gradual outgrowth of constructive study of the accumulated sorted facts, empirically verified over a period of time, until consistent generalizations or logical principles can be formulated." *Arnold Rose* defined a theory as, "an integrated body of definitions, assumptions and general propositions covering a given subject matter from which a comprehensive and consistent set of specific and testable (Principles) can be deducted logically." He characterizes a theory as, 'one in which: *(a)* definitions, assumptions and general propositions are consistent in so far as possible with careful, though not always systematic, observations, *(b)* a minimum number of definitions and general propositions are made *(c)* deducted hypotheses are in readily testable form". From the above definitions we can draw the followings features of a theory:

1. Theory is the result of continued study of facts.
2. It is tested or studied over a period of time till it is accepted as a theory.
3. Generalizations and principles are formulated while constructing a theory.

Purpose of Theory

Theory building is a part of social research and social scientists have laboured hard through centuries to build theories in various social sciences. As the very purpose of social research is to study human behaviour, it also becomes the very purpose of theory. Theory should not only study the human behaviour but also it must explain the relationship between various variables. Theory must also serve to predict the behaviour of human beings, and explain the courses. The explanation may be in the form of statements. Human behaviour and their inter-relationship of a set circumstance may vary to other and a theory can help to compare places and circumstances.

Theory and Hypothesis

Hypothesis, when tested and proved the next obvious stage is formation of theory. Hence, there is a close link between hypothesis and theory. *Young* has rightly observed that "a hypothesis is generally formulated before the facts are verified. It deals with a comparatively narrow range of facts, it is a preliminary assumption adopted for the explanation of facts which have been observed only in cursory manner. A theory on the other hand, is a generalization arrived at after verification and it deals with a broader range of facts. It is often said that a theory is "an elaborate and tested hypothesis."

Role of Theory

Theory has a greater role to play in society. For social scientists and social researchers it is of immense value and it gives an orientation to them. A researcher who has grip over theories of his field can formulate hypothesis easily and he can proceed his research in order and smoothly. *Goode and Hatt* explain the role of theory as follows:

Theory as Orientation

These veterans feel that theory 'narrows the range of facts to be studied'. Any phenomenon or problem can be studied in different ways. What is needed and what is not needed can be oriented properly by theory. Beating round the bush can be avoided. "Each science and each specialization with a broader field abstracts from reality, keeping its attention upon a few aspects of given phenomena rather than upon all aspects. Only thus can the work of science be reduced to manageability. The board orientation of each field, then "focuses upon a limited range of things while ignoring or making assumptions about others."

Theory as Conceptualization and Classification

Terms and concepts that are commonly used must be defined properly in order to understand their range, depth, implication and connotations. This is called as conceptualization and classification. Theory helps the researcher to define them and classify them properly. Every science is organized by a structure of concepts, which refer to the major processes and objects to be studied. It is the relationships between these concepts which are stated in 'the facts of science'. Such terms make up the specialized vocabulary that the scientist uses normally. It is clear that if knowledge is to be organized, there must be some systems imposed upon the facts which are observable. As a consequence, a major task in any science is the development of systems of classification, a structure of concepts, and an increasingly precise set of definitions for these terms.

The Task of Summarizing

Another important role of theory is to summarize what is already known about the object of study. Summarizing of facts is necessary to arrive at generalizations and to find out relationships between variables.

Theory Predicts Facts

If theory summarizes facts and states a general uniformity beyond the immediate observations, it also becomes a 'prediction of facts'. By predicting facts through theory, it acts as guideline for the researcher to collect data and to shape his research.

Theory Points to Gaps in Our Knowledge

Like predicting the facts, theory identifies the gaps that have been left by others or in the particular area of research.

3

Hypothesis

Formulation of hypothesis and its verification are the fundamental aspects of research. A hypothesis is a hunch or belief or speculation about a phenomenon. It is based on common sense, theory or empirical facts. Scientific research is mostly understood today as a process of forming hypothesis and checking it by means of observed data. The observed data is found to be inconsistent with the hypothesis, the hypothesis is rejected and if there is an agreement it is accepted. Thus, when a proposition is tested, it reinforces the theory.

Definition

Goode and Scates: "A hypothesis is a shrewd guess or inference that formulated and provisionally adopted to explain observed facts or conditions and to guide in further investigation."

Walter R. Brog: "Hypotheses reflect the research worker's guess as to the probable outcome of his experiment and they place clear and specific goals before the researcher and provide him with a basis for selecting sample and research procedures to meet these goals."

Rummel: "A Statement capable of being tested and thereby verified or rejected."

Goode and Hatt: "A hypothesis states what we are looking for. What facts are assembled; ordered and seen in a relationship, they constitute a theory. The theory is not speculation, but built upon fact. Now the various facts in a theory may be logically analyzed, and relationships other than those stated in the theory can be deduced. At this point there is no knowledge as to whether such deductions are correct. The formation of deduction however constitutes a hypothesis, if verified it becomes a part of a future theoretical construction."

M.H. Gopal: "It has been defined as a tentative solution posed on a cursory observation of known and available data, and adopted provisionally to explain certain events and to guide in the investigation of others. It is in fact, a possible solution to the problem."

Functions of Hypothesis

From the above definitions we are able to infer three main functions of hypothesis. They are: *(1)* To test theories *(2)* To Suggest theories *(3)* To describe social phenomena.

To Test Theories

The relationship between theory and hypothesis is very close indeed. Theories are based on facts, which if elaborated becomes hypothesis. Theories need to be tested in as a tool of explanation for some events. The theories lend themselves for empirical test only if the facts, proposition and assumptions implied in them are split up into specific hypothesis.

To Suggest Theories

Another function of hypothesis is to suggest theories. Theory is derived out of hypothesis and is considered as elaborate hypothesis. In other words hypothesis when refined becomes a theory. *Carter V. Good* observes that, "there is no sharp line of demarcation between hypothesis and theory, since the basic difference is one of complexity and the extent of testing against the evidence. In its early stages or testing a theory usually has been called as hypothesis checked against the data and their logical implications towards a successful conclusion, it may become known as a theory." *Goode & Hatt* say that "every worth while theory permits the formulation of additional hypothesis. These, when tested, are either proved or disproved and in turn constitute further tests of the original theory."

To Describe Social Phenomena

When a hypothesis is tested, it explains the phenomenon associated with it. This phenomenon may be new or not known earlier. Neither a theory nor a hypothesis is involved in such test. Any common sense knowledge or belief is put to empirical test to determine its validity. Hence, new knowledge is gathered. *Goode and Hatt* observe that, "a hypothesis looks forward. It may prove to be correct or incorrect. On any event the hypothesis is a question put in such a way that answer of some kind can be forthcoming."

Importance of Hypothesis

In addition to putting the theory to test, a hypothesis has to perform certain other functions. In many ways, it is a guiding point to a research. *Young* observes that "formulation of the hypothesis gives definite point to the enquiry, aids in establishing direction in which to proceed and helps to delimit the field of inquiry by singling out the pertinent facts on which to concentrate and by determining which facts should be set aside, at least for the time being. The use of hypothesis thus prevents a blind search and indiscriminate gathering of data which may later prove irrelevant to the problem under study." Hence, to collect the needed data hypothesis serves as a forerunner of time and keep the research away from considerable amount of confusion. *Prof. Northtrop* also views that, the functions of hypothesis is to direct research for finding out order among facts. The suggestions formulated in any hypothesis may be solutions to the problems.

Hypotheses have also certain practical values to society. Besides serving as a means for seeking solution to various social problems, they help in understanding the social phenomena in their proper perspective and refute certain 'common sense' notions about human behaviour.

Types of Hypotheses

Descriptive Hypotheses

These are propositions that describe the characteristics (such as size, form or distribution) of a variable. The variable may be an object, person, organization, situation or event. Some examples are:

1. "The rate of unemployment in India is higher than that of USA."
2. "Public Enterprises are more amenable for Centralized Planning".

Relational Hypotheses

These are propositions which describe the relationship between two variables. The relationship suggested may be positive or negative correlation or causal relationship. Some examples are:

1. "Families with higher incomes spend more for recreation."
2. "Upper-class people have fewer children than lower class people."

Causal hypotheses state that the existence of, or a change in, one variable causes or leads to an effect on another variable, and the latter becomes the dependent variable.

Working Hypotheses

While planning the study of a problem, hypotheses are formed. Initially they may not be very specific. In such cases, they are referred to as, 'working hypotheses' which are subject to modification as the investigation proceeds.

Null Hypotheses

These are hypnotically framed statements denying what are explicitly indicated in working hypotheses. They do not, nor were ever intended to exist in reality.

They state that no difference exists between the parameter and the statistic being compared to it. For example, even though there is a relationship between a family's income and expenditure on recreation, a null hypothesis may state: "There is no relationship between families income level and expenditure on recreation."

Null hypotheses are more exact. It is easier to reject the contrary of an hypothesis than to confirm it with complete certainty. Hence, the concept of null hypotheses is found to be very useful.

Statistical Hypotheses

These are statements about a statistical population. These are derived from a sample. These are quantitative in nature in that they are numerically measurable, e.g., "Group A is older than Group B"

Common Sense Hypotheses

These represent the common sense ideas. They state the existence of empirical uniformities perceived through day to day observations. Much empirical uniformity may be observed in business establishments, the social background of workers, and the behaviour patterns of specific groups like students, e.g., "shop-assistants in small shops lack motivation".

Complex Hypotheses

These aim at testing the existence of logically derived relationships between empirical uniformities. For example, in the early stage human ecology described empirical uniformities in the distribution of land value, industrial concentrations, type of business and other phenomena.

Analytical Hypotheses

These are concerned with the relationship of analytic variables. These hypotheses occur at the highest level of abstraction. These specify relationship between changes in one property and changes in another. For example, the study of human fertility might show empirical regularities by wealth, education, region and religion.

This level of hypothesizing is the most sophisticated mode of formulation and contributes to the development of 'brilliant' abstract theories.

Characteristics of Hypothesis

Goode & Hatt in their book, "Methods in Social Research", discuss the following characteristics of hypothesis:

Hypothesis Must be Defined Clearly

The definition should be commonly accepted. Further these definitions should be communicable rather than be the product of a 'private world'.

Hypothesis Should Have Empirical Reference

Scientific concept must have an ultimate empirical reference. No working hypothesis can embody moral judgments. Such statements as "Criminals are no worse than businessmen" are no more usable or working hypothesis. In other words, while a hypothesis may study value judgments, such a goal must be separated from a moral preachment or plea for acceptance of ones values.

The Hypothesis Must be Specific

The operations and predications indicated by it should be spelt out. The possibility of actually testing the hypothesis can be appraised. Hence, it must be specific in terms of its purpose, clarity and testability. Such specific formulations have the advantage of assuring that research is practical and significant.

Hypothesis Should be related to Available Techniques

These are some aspects of the hypothesis which may make its formulation worth while. If the problem is significant enough as a possible frame of reference it may be useful whether or not it can be tested at the time. So a researcher must review the articles on the subject being studied and prepare a list of various techniques used. If one is unable to find any discussion on techniques, it is better to make a research on the necessary techniques.

The Hypothesis Should be Related to a Body of Theory

Any research must help to refute qualify or support any existing theory or social relation. A science can be cumulative only by building on an existing body of fact and theory. It cannot develop if each study is an isolated survey.

Origin of Hypothesis

As society grows, cultural patterns continue to change and socio-economic milieu undergoes a constant transformation. Such changes in socio-economic relations, human behaviour, values and attitudes provide ample scope for identification of hypothesis.

1. The General Culture in which a Science develops, furnishes many of its Basic Hypothesis

Cultural values serve to direct research interests. Today's science has developed to a great dimension due to the function of culture. Folk wisdom also serves as another source of hypotheses. For example, in Western society race is thought to be an important determinant of human behaviour. This can be used to frame hypotheses.

2. Hypotheses Originate in the Science Itself

Scientists continuously discuss current research and through it, important areas for further research are located. Through these interaction modes of thought, concepts and problems develop. These in turn suggest further hypotheses.

3. Analogies are often a Source of Useful Hypotheses

The success of a system in one discipline can be used in other discipline also. The hypotheses that resulted in the development of human ecology, for example, were an application of established theory in the field of plant and animal ecology.

4. Hypotheses are also the Consequence of personal, idiosyncratic experience

Not only do culture, science and analogy attract the formulation of hypotheses but also the way in which the individual reacts to each of these is also a factor in the statement of hypotheses. Therefore, the individual experience of the scientists contributes to the hypotheses.

Testing of Hypothesis

Knowledge or a fact could be accepted only when it has validity. The validity of such knowledge could be accepted only when it is tested with regard to its usefulness or truth. Hence, to accept hypotheses, which are merely hunches or guesses, as facts, they are to be tested. Testing hypotheses means subjecting them to some sort of empirical scrutiny to determine if they are supported or refuted by what the researcher observes.

Robert Bales states that the following questions should be asked about hypotheses before they are tested:

1. Are the terms, empirically specific, so that the concepts or variables can be distinguished in concrete situations?
2. Is the relationship between variables such that it could be verified or nullified by means of empirical operations?
3. Is there any prior evidence as to the truth or falseness of the relationship?
4. Can an appropriate study design be devised?
5. Are the variables context-bound (e.g., restricted to play group or gang) or could they be equally well

applied to other interaction situations (e.g., work group or family)?

6. Are the generalizations 'culture-bound' or can they be also applied realistically to other cultures?
7. If other relevant factors or subject to change in the course of the observations, are they adequately specified and enumerated, so that the observer can ascertain whether, they have changed during the period of observation?
8. Is the generalization a part of the theoretical system from which it could be deducted as well as being verified by the proposed empirical induction?
9. Is the empirical system that is constructed sufficiently precise and articulates to permit predictions in concrete situations?

Black and Champion, in their book, "Methods and Issues in Social Research," specify two prerequisites to test hypotheses which are given below:

1. A real social situation is needed that will suffice as a reasonable testing ground for the hypotheses.
2. The investigator should make sure that the hypotheses are testable.

After these conditions are fulfilled the researcher collects data, processes them and based on these findings he has to support or refute the hypotheses. Unbiased judgment and professional ethics are the guiding principles to avoid subjectivity.

Problems in Formulating Hypotheses

A researcher has to come across several problems in formulating hypotheses. It is as difficult as finding out a research problem or identifying a suitable theory. The following are some of the difficulties in formulating hypotheses as pointed out by *Goode and Hatt* in their book, "Methods in Social Research".

1. Absence of a theoretical framework.

2. Lack of ability to utilize the theoretical frame work logically.
3. Failure to acquaint with available research techniques so as to above to phrase the hypotheses properly.

The researcher must bear in mind that he has to formulate a good, definite, and testable hypothesis. At the beginning stage, when one is not familiar with various processes of research, the formulation of a sound hypothesis would be somewhat difficult. He may frame some formulations, and can say that they are hypotheses. But they may not have the testability.

Is Hypothesis Necessary?

This is a controversial issue; and there is no categorical opinion on this. Hypotheses give purpose and direction to the research. One of the main objectives of hypothesis is to test a theory as well as to formulate a theory. When we have adequate theory in a science the need to formulate a hypothesis is sometimes questioned. *M.H. Gopal* in his book, "An Introduction to Research Procedure in Social Sciences" says that while hypothesis is useful it is not always indispensable. In physical sciences which are very highly developed, the hypothesis is most often necessary. In social sciences, research may be conducted without formulating hypotheses. Only in certain types of studies hypotheses are needed. *P.V. Young* also holds the same view.

SECTION – II

TYPES AND METHODS OF RESEARCH

4

Types of Research

Social research has been classified in several ways depending on the purpose for which it is undertaken, the extent to which it satisfies the scientific procedures or the method of collection of data, the control factor involved and the purpose of research. There is no hard and fast rule in the classification. It is more for the sake of promoting better understanding or for the sake of convenience. The classifications are not mutually exclusive and often overlap. There are several ways of classification of research on the basis of field, purpose, place, method of data collection, application and control factor (See chart).

Types of Research

The common way of classifying social research is on the basis of the purpose for which it is conducted, or its application value. Four major types of Research namely, Pure Research, Applied Research, Action Research and Evaluation Research fall under this category.

Various Types of Research—Why?

As knowledge is expanding new problems are confronted by researchers, presuming that old problems have been settled or solutions have been found for old problems. Fresh problems may start from old problems are a fresh or due to the proliferation of knowledge. Mankind has to answer questions that are raised very often and such answers must be in the form of solutions. A problem can be attacked from many angles and many researchers may try to find a solution to a single problem when it becomes a daring necessity. For example research on controlling AIDS is undertaken in all countries and by very many researchers as it is threatening the social and cultural fabric of each society. Here the challenge is to find a solution to this menace. In which country you are doing research on AIDS or in which language your are doing research have become secondary one.

By having one type of research we cannot find solutions to unsolved questions, because problems in social research are not the same and have various dimensions. Even after thousands of years of human civilization we are in position only to answer a few questions. There are thousands of questions unanswered or thousands of social problems yet to be given solution. Further social science problems are related to happenings which may be past, present or future. Having one method of research we cannot study all social problems. Hence:

1. Various methods of research in social science is needed to study and find solutions to various social problems which may have various dimensions.
2. When society grows or changes, problems are ought to arise very often. Such problems may be new one or old one. We need different yardsticks to measure such problems.
3. Having one method or type of research we cannot study a problem relating to a past as well as present. Likewise having one method of research one cannot study a social problem relating to the present and future.
4. Hence, we have different types of social research to study social problems relating to the past, present and future.

5. In sciences other than social sciences we can accurately predict the future. But in social science research prediction or forecasting is little difficult as this field of research deals with human behaviour, which is unpredicted and not constant. Even this difficulty is overcome now by means of introducing new tools in social research.

P.V. Young's observation is worth quoting here. She says, "no single scientific technique in gathering and analyzing data would suffice. Research studies generally utilize not only a variety of techniques but approach the subject matter from a variety of viewpoints. This procedure rests on the assumption that no one point of view or scientific discipline can encompass total social reality. Neither should a single technique of study be regarded as sovereign."

Pure Research

Pure research or fundamental research is the research that is understood in its most original and formal sense. It draws its pattern and spirit from physical sciences and has represented a rigorous structured type of analysis. Gathering knowledge for knowledge sake is termed as pure or basic research. Many scientific inventions such as invention of steam engine or invention of electricity fall under this category. Several economic theories like consumers' surplus and indifference curve analysis also belong to this category.

Pure research is undertaken for widening the horizon of knowledge. 'Knowledge for the Knowledge sake' is the watchword of pure research. It is conceived as a search for broad principles and syntheses without any immediate utilitarian objective. It is more an intellectual exploration arising from insatiable intellectual curiosity. The finding of the fundamental research has little concern for immediate application, though in the long run it may have greater utility. It is theoretical in nature and its essential element is building theories and principles by broad generalization. The outcome of the pure research has universal application. This kind of research employs rigorous sampling procedure in order to extend the findings beyond the group or situation studied. It also helps in construction of research tools and their refinement. It is time consuming and involves much cost. A researcher may have to devote his entire life time, out of scientific curiosity unmindful of immediate rewards. The sphere of activity of fundamental research is extraordinarily wide.

In the present state of social sciences, research and theory are not always closely linked, and theories are likely to contain speculative elements. Instead of telling theories the social research has to contribute more often to the development of theory than to its testing.

Aims of Pure Research

Goode and Hatt list the following aims of Pure Research:

1. By developing general principles, theory offers solutions to many practical problems.
2. Pure research helps to find the central factors in a practical problem.
3. Research as an answer to problems may become a standard procedure for the administrator.
4. Theoretical research develops many alternative solutions, with the result that alternative costs may be weighed and ultimately reduced.

Features of Pure Research

General Principles

General principles are the quintessence of knowledge and form the basis or foundation for any field of knowledge. Without framing general principles a discipline or knowledge cannot be expanded or elaborated. Principles are also the basic yardsticks to measure the growth of knowledge in a particular field. General principles are core to pure research.

Central Factors

Any social or economic or cultural problem would be surrounded by certain key factors. Pure research helps to locate such key. For example poverty being a practical problem may be the result of certain key factors like illiteracy, big family, unemployment, etc. *Goode and Hatt* say "all too often those who adopt a common sense approach see the problem in traditional ways and fail to abstract the key factors. As a consequences, the solution is likely to be an inefficient one."

Standard Procedure

By building new theories solutions to problems become a standardized one. "Pure research may have an effect upon the pattern of administrative procedure, as the practitioner learns of its utility. This development has not been a common one, but both Government and business organizations have begun to utilize 'Research and Planning units' to evaluate the techniques which have been applied in the past and to develop new solutions to old as well as new problems. The pattern of pure research has an effect upon the solutions of practical problems in that its aims and procedures become the usual, long term approach to the latter type of problem."

Alternative Solutions and Cost

In the initial stage the cost on pure research may look heavy, but in the long run the benefits will neutralize the cost. "The solutions that theoretical research first develops are likely to be very expensive. Most of the applications of science which have become common in our civilization—radio, television, were originally laboratory appliances, unwisely, costly and inefficient. However, pure science characteristically continues the investigation beyond a workable solution to more precise generalizations, discovery of the essential factors, and ascertainment of the exact conditions under which the process operates. Consequently, after a time there are many solutions for a given type of problem, with different main and subsidiary consequences. We are thus permitted to choose the best solution for our practical problem."

Applied Research

The fundamental research interests only a fewer scientists, and it does not make contributions to development at grass root level. More scientists started evincing interest in applied research due to the limitations in basic research such as cost and time involved and lack of basic research tradition particularly in developing countries. According to *P.V. Young* "gathering knowledge that could aid in the betterment of human destiny is termed 'applied' or practical research."

The applied research is a development aid and is directed towards the development of human society. It is need based and aims at solving immediate problems. It is completed in a short span of time. Its findings are evaluated on the basis of local applicability, not in terms of universal validity. It is empirical and man-centered. Its major purpose is to improve the system or practice and the theoretical development is of minor importance. This method provides sufficient flexibility to permit modification of hypotheses and procedures as the study goes on. While analyzing the problem it synthesizes the approaches developed by different social sciences.

Between pure and applied research neither there is conflict nor there sharp line of difference. Each contributes for the other and they cross fertilize. Both are important for the development.

"Basic research resembles the sowing whilst the judging of practical problems can be compared with harvesting." Applied research is more relevant in developing countries like India, where there is a multitude of pressing social problems. Practically all social sciences research undertaken in India are applied or action research which aid in the formulation of policy. According to *M.H. Gopal,* "Unapplied knowledge is the knowledge short of its meaning." A great service that research can render is to study the practical and real problems facing backward societies. It calls for integration between the two. A researcher has to recognize the bearing of his work on the inter-relation between theory and applications. If the researcher concentrates on applied research, he must examine its relevance to social theory if its potential contribution is to be realized. If his major interest is in the development of social theory, he must take into account ways of testing and expanding his theory by empirical research if it is to become more than interesting speculation.

Stouffer in his study on "After thoughts of a contributor to the American Soldier", points out the contributions of applied research to social science:

1. By providing the kind of convincing evidence of the usefulness to society which is necessary to continuing support.
2. By utilizing and developing techniques which can also be made to serve the so called basic research.
3. By providing data and idea which may speed up the process of generalization.

Aims of Applied Research

Goode and Hatt list the following aims of applied research:

Applied Research Can Contribute New Facts

New facts may come out with the result of new works undertaken by scientists. "New facts may lead to the initiation, rejection and reformulation of theory or to its clarification and redefinition."

Applied Research Can Put Theory to The Test

Applied research offers an opportunity to test the validity of existing theory. It attempts the diagnosis of a situation and a solution."

Applied Research May Aid in Conceptual Clarification

Often concepts have become unclear and need clarification. Different interpretation by different people leads to confusion. Applied research can help to clarity concepts. "A concept exhibits its vagueness most sharply when we begin to define the procedures and operations for dealing with it in research."

Applied Research May Integrate Previously Existing Theory

The solution to a problem may require integration of many theoretical as well as applied investigations in several fields. Applied research can easily integrate theories.

DIFFERENCE BETWEEN PURE RESEARCH AND APPLIED RESEARCH

PURE RESEARCH	APPLIED RESEARCH
1. It is undertaken primarily for gathering knowledge and is based on the assumption that all knowledge is potentially useful.	It is utilitarian and is primarily undertaken for the betterment of humanity. Knowledge is applied to concrete problem.
2. The sphere of activity of pure research is wide. It is broad based and more abstract in nature.	Applied research is confined to narrow fields and is more specific in nature.
3. It involves long-term, protracted and time consuming process.	It is short-term, time bound and result oriented.
4. It involves huge financial outlay.	The financial outlay is relatively limited.
5. It aims at understanding the social phenomenon i.e., diagnostic.	It aims at finding solution to social problems i.e., therapeutic.
6. Pure research takes up problems understood by scientists i.e., it is scholastic and elitist in nature.	Problems understood by common people are the subject matter of applied research.
7. Pure research is based on theoretical abstractions and speculations.	It is based on practical application and empirical method.
8. Pure research aims at developing theories by discovering broad generalization or principles.	Applied research is need based and is applied to immediate problem solving effort i.e., ameliorative.

(i) Problem Oriented Research

One of the classifications of social research is 'problem oriented research.' Any research is problem oriented. A researcher can come across problems during the course of his research or he can seek the very problems for the sake of it. In such research the duty of the researcher would be to devote more of his attention towards magnifying the problem rather than finding solution to such problem. One can find problems from an issue or from a phenomenon or from a happening. Culling out the crux of the issues, which are amenable for research itself is a task and forms part of finding a problem. All problems cannot be considered to be research problems or all problems will not have the properties of a problem. In otherwords any social problem worth studying must have 'viability'. It should enthuse the researcher to kindle his originality and must create a 'curiosity about unknown'. The problem must also be pragmatic and must have 'social relevance'. It should not stop with satisfying the ego of the researcher. The problem must also lead him to come out with pragmatic solutions.

A problem can be called as a research problem only when it satisfies the following conditions:

1. The problem must have viability of potentiality to stand as a research problem. It should satisfy the norms of scientific inquiry.
2. The problem must have social relevance. The study should be useful to the society and must draw the attention off all concerned.
3. As far as possible a research problem must be 'virgin' in nature and must not be touched by others. So the researcher must find out the gap in his area of research.
4. There must be 'felt need' for research over the problem. Such problem must be in need of further elaboration and exploration. A compelling situation must arise to study a problem.
5. A research problem must come out with pragmatic solutions to the issues. The user of the problem must be many.
6. A social research problem must be upto date or relevant to the current social happenings.

While selecting a 'problem oriented research' the researcher can consult experts of the field, policy makers and researchers who are doing research already in the field. Duplication of work must be avoided.

(ii) Performance Evaluation Studies

Such type of research studies are the outcome of our planned economic development. After the Second World War, Governments have started vying with each other in proclaiming themselves as Welfare Governments. Such Welfare Governments have started spending more money for public welfare and economic development. Expenditure through five year plans forms primary one among all other expenditures. As huge money is spent on public welfare, it has become necessary to evaluate the benefits of such expenditures. According to *Baker,* "the purpose of evaluation research is to evaluate some social activity, which has been set up to address and ameliorate a social problem." The objectives of performance evaluation studies are:

1. To know whether the money is spent as per the guidelines laid down.
2. To know whether the priority in outlay has been given to the pressing socio-economic problems.
3. In the case of industrial and agricultural outlays, whether importance is given to lay down the infrastructure development, thereby in the long run the country should attain self sufficient in basic needs.
4. In the case of technology development, whether we can match the speed of advanced countries and keep up the tempo of growth continuously.
5. To evaluate each programmes and to verify whether the programmes have benefited for whom they have been introduced.
6. To find out the pitfalls that comes across in implementing programmes.
7. Whether the schemes have been implemented through the course laid down or any deviation occurred?

Areas of Performance Evaluation Studies

Performance Evaluation studies are conducted on the following socio-economic areas:

1. Field of Agriculture

Agriculture being the primary sector of our economy, it is necessary to see that it is contributing its share to the national wealth and income. We have to verify whether agriculture is doing justice to its dependents by way of increasing their income. It is also necessary to verify whether the input industry is set on the right lines and farmers are able to get needed inputs like seeds, fertilizers, pesticides and machineries for the right price.

2. Field of Industry

Industry being the prime mover of the economy must solve economic problems like unemployment, scarcity of goods, earning of foreign exchange problems like unemployment, scarcity of goods, etc. Evaluation is needed on the above fields and based on the evaluation studies remedial measures must by suggested to solve the problem faced by industries.

3. Poverty Alleviation Schemes

Government has introduced various poverty alleviation schemes at State and Central levels. Such schemes are subsidized by the tax payers' money. Hence, it is necessary to evaluate the efficiency of such schemes and to ascertain whether the benefits have reached the right people. IRDP and PDS are such programmes which need continuous evaluation and monitoring.

4. Welfare Schemes

Welfare schemes like health, sanitation, housing, environmental protection, etc., have occupied important place in the public expenditure of developed as well as developing countries. Evaluation studies are needed to increase the quality and quantity of such schemes to all citizens.

5. *Educational Schemes*

Countries like ours have invested heavily on education from primary level to universities level. Education is made compulsory to all citizens and is made free upto a level. Such costs are borne by the State and expenditure made on various heads must be evaluated to know whether we are able to remove illiteracy, whether depressed sections have been access to professional education, whether the type of education that we impart is relevant to the society and whether we are keeping pace with the advanced countries in improving the quality of our education.

Type of Evaluation Studies

There are three types of evaluation studies:

Periodic Evaluation

This evaluation is undertaken giving an interval say one year, two years or five years. As prescribed gap is allowed we can detect deviations or loopholes and can rectify them in the next evaluation.

Concurrent Evaluation

Such studies are a continuous process and are akin to social audit. Mistakes or deviations can be found out and feedback could be provided to correct deviations.

Terminal Evaluation

Such studies are undertaken after a project or scheme is over. There is little scope to correct deviations under such studies. But such studies would be useful when new schemes are launched.

Baker (doing social research) gives four types of Evaluation Research:

(i) *On-going Programme Evaluation:* This is undertaken

simultaneously when the programme is going on.

(ii) *Cost Benefit Analysis:* This seeks to assess whether the benefit of a programme or social strategy is worth its cost.

(iii) *Community Impact Assessment:* This is to find out the effect of a new policy on the community.

(iv) *Time-Series Analysis:* Evaluating a programme after every particular interval.

(iii) Impact Studies

Impact studies are those studies which are undertaken to study the positive or negative results of certain variables. The effect of adding a variable or the effect of eliminating a variable is studied. Impact studies are also undertaken to find out the results or effects of a scheme before it was introduced and after it was introduced. It is also undertaken to know the position before and after a particular period of year.

Variables and Impact

Studying of one type of variable or the other is a social process and research studies can point out the type of impact or the level of impact. In social research two types of variables are available for researchers, namely independent variables and dependent variables.

Independent variables cause effect or impact over dependent variable. One or more independent variable can cause effect on a dependent variable. Age, income, size or the family, size of land holdings, etc. are independent variables. Phenomena like savings, expenditure, borrowings, repayment etc., are dependent variables. Usually one dependent variable is caused or affected by one or more independent variables.

Impact 'Before' and 'After' a Scheme

Second type of impact studies are undertaken while a scheme is introduced. When a scheme is introduced the socio-economic conditions that prevailed before the introduction of the scheme were measured, quantified and noted with statistical details. After the introduction of the scheme due gap is given say two years, five years or ten years. Then again the socio-economic changes are measured as to know whether the scheme has produced any results positive or negative. To improve the living conditions of weaker sections many schemes are introduced. Through impact studies we can know the benefits of such schemes on such groups.

Impact Over a Period

By choosing a particular year as 'Base Year' we can study the impact of schemes before and after that period. Socio-economic developments are studied before and after our independence.

Uses of Impact Studies

Impact studies have the following uses:

1. For planners and policy makers such studies help to understand the effects of specific programmes implemented.
2. Through such studies we can identify the factors which contributed to the success of a scheme or which have not contributed anything or which have negatively contributed to the growth.
3. When a new product is introduced in the market, impact of it on other products or existing products could be studied and later a safer passage could be introduced.
4. If a company wants to increase its market share, it can be done so through the results of impact studies.

(iv) Action Research

Action research or policy research, as it is sometimes called, is a type of applied research. There is thin line of difference between the two. Though several authors consider both these types of research as one and the same, social scientists have differentiated action research from the larger field of applied research. Action research aims at contributing to the practical concerns of the people in an immediate problematic situation. It not only aims at discovering new facts, but helps in altering certain conditions, experienced by the community as unsatisfactory. Another significant feature of action research is that it is frequently carried out on the request of a client organization that hopes to solve some problem. The action research is carried out in the setting of a functional organization. As against the 'neutral' and 'objective' elements of classical research, action research is less elitist and provides for intervention, and participation to bring about certain desired changes.

There is close collaboration between the sponsoring organization and the research agency. The organization, sponsoring the research to some extent participates in planning and carrying out the research. In the action research the theory is not only tested and applied in a given set of conditions, it is also modified according to the local prevailing conditions. It adapts to the local prevailing conditions and change that takes place in the community. The action research makes full use of the available materials on fundamental and applied research and helps in testing the hypothesis in the varying field situations as well as formulation of new hypothesis.

Definition and Meaning of Action Research

Stephen M. Corey of Columbia University, an authority of this subject defines Action Research as "an attempt to get the scientific approach to practical problems used at the grass root level".

Action Research is a type of evaluation study. It is launched to solve a problem or for improving the existing situation.

Features of Action Research

1. It is nothing but bringing a trained mind on the solution of problems in our day to day life situations.
2. It can be applied to a variety of situations such as class room teaching, management, social work, extension work etc.
3. It enables one to think better to identify problems and analyze the reasons for them and to solve them.
4. Action research seeks to bridge the gap between theory and practice, knowledge and behaviour.
5. It is more effective and easy to administer.
6. It is less elitist and provides for intervention and participation.
7. It makes full use of the available materials on pure and applied research and helps in testing hypothesis in the varying field situations as well as formulation of new hypothesis.

Objectives of Action Research

1. To find immediate solutions to problems by being pragmatic in approach.
2. To discover new facts by altering certain conditions based on practical experience.
3. To test a theory and if possible to modify it according to local conditions.

Starting Point of Action Research

Unlike other methods of research, availability of time is a constraint for Action Research. The researcher has very less time at his disposal. Hence, he is in a position to give a quick start to his work. But at the same time he must be cautious in the quality of wok and outcome of his research. Hence, he must make a cautious and at the same time purposeful starting.

'Self Questioning' and resultant 'Genuine Discontent' is the starting point of actions research. Smug self-satisfaction is a sure sign of stagnation and stunted growth. On the other hand 'self dissatisfaction' based on the learning desire for self improvement is a most valuable attitude and guide. In the words of *Peter Drucker,* such genuine discontent is "the most real expression of pride in job and work and of responsibility". Responsibility, not smug satisfaction, is the only thing that will serve. To perform one has to take responsibility for one's own actions and their impact. Action research serves this objective of peak performance eminently well.

Action Research Design

Action Research has the following steps:

1. The first step is to identify the problem area.
2. The second step is to pinpoint a problem.
3. The third step is to identify the problem causes or the problem. This is known as 'Problem Analysis', and much importance is attached to this step in Action Research.
4. The fourth step is Action Hypothesis. It must be related to Action Research which the researcher wants to take. It should be based on central not peripheral causes. One must be specific about what one want to do and be clear about what might happen.
5. The fifth step is framing Action Research Design. This consists of *(a)* Base line data *(b)* Sources of data, *(c)* Tools for data and *(d)* Action Programme and Time chart.
6. The sixth step is the periodic assessment of Action Research project.
7. The last step is the Evaluation of the project. This is a very important stage and Action Research studies the following questions as proposed by *Proscot Hinkle:*

   (i) What is it that has changed?

   (ii) How much has it changed (extent)?

   (iii) How quickly has it changed (rate)?

(iv) What where the conditions before and after the change?

(v) What occurred during the transition?

(vi) What was the stimuli that induced change?

(vii) Through what mechanisms did change occur?

(viii) What brought stabilization at a particular point in change?

(ix) Can directionality be observed in the change?

These questions indicated the problem areas which can be the focus of evaluation. These areas are:

(a) Impact of the programme on intended recipients.

(b) Extent of the programmes effect on the intended recipients.

(c) Time involved in bringing about the impact of effects.

(d) Before-after measures of the variables which are supposed to undergo change.

(e) Identification of the events and processes that took place between the before-and after-measures.

(f) Analysis of the subject-matter or content of the programme.

(g) Organizational, structural and operational aspects of the programme.

(h) Factors in the change introduced.

(i) Direction of the changes observed relative to the objectives of the programme.

Criteria for Action Research

The common criteria for a good Action Research Design could be:

(a) It must be sufficiently specific so as to enable to take action immediately.

(b) It must be such that it could be completed within a couple of months.

(c) If must be such that the research could be completed with the available facilities.

(d) It must be such that the cooperation of people concerned is easily available.

(e) It must be clearly related to one of the causes.

(f) It should be such that it does not isolate the administrative requirements.

(g) The success of Action Research depends on the coordination and rapport of the sponsoring agency with the research agency.

(h) The method of investigation adopted in Action Research must be suitable to the filed situation by integrating local knowledge in the research process.

(v) Feasibility Studies

While analyzing the scope for starting new firms or organizations, we have to think scientifically about the scope, viability, survival instincts, etc. of the proposed unit. Such scientific assessment can be provided by a "Feasibility study". A feasibility study can predict the success or failure of an organization. A feasibility study can assess the deposit and other resource potential of a proposed bank. The level of competition and strategies to woo the customers can also be drawn. It can also fix indicators for success like break even analysis, credit deposit ratio, profit ratio etc. A feasibility study can not lead us to failure. A ten per cent margin of probability of success or failure can be given. A cent per cent success of the study can be ensured provided the implementers take the scope, suggestions and strategies true to the spirit of the feasibility study.

Feasibility studies are essential in the field of industries. "Feasibility studies indeed have gained considerable importance in recent years especially in developing countries seeking to harvest their natural resources for rapid industrial development. In fact prospective entrepreneurs like very much to know and perhaps, the various aspects of their selected industry before investing their capital in such a venture. Sufficient and requisite knowledge of feasibility studies may help them immensely in this regard. Such studies also help the promotional agencies to know the viability of a proposed industrial venture so that they may counsel prospective entrepreneurs better.

Moreover, if some of the personnel of the promotional agencies learn how to make feasibility studies, then it may create confidence in them as they would be collecting all the particulars concerning a particular industry. The confidence, in turn, will help them to convince others.

Feasibility Studies Would Then Help the Following

(i) Persons interested in starting industries but appear to be baffled to identify the product and/or products to be produced by them;

(ii) Persons who are already in the industry line i.e., they have already been entrepreneurs but are interested to have entry into new lines of products, products of which they like to make a systematic study that will help them to know whether new entry/entries would be economically viable or not;

(iii) State and Central Government proposing to start new industries specially in backward areas may do it well to undertake feasibility studies to examine the strength or weaknesses of their proposals because large public money may be involved in the process and hence, a prior thorough study to examine economic feasibility in this regard may be highly desirable.

(iv) Different departments/institutions/organizations etc., in the State as well as in the Centre that connected with economic and or industrial development in the country may undertake feasibility studies to prepare a list of identified products which may be economically viable and the same may be handed over to the prospective entrepreneurs so that they may examine the product or products which they may like to start to be produced in their new enterprises. Such a list may be of immense value to the prospective entrepreneurs in identifying their products.

(v) Consultancy organizations may be developed to be specialized in the technique of feasibility studies and such a specialized skill may be sold to the customers to ease out their problems of identifying the product/products specially because such an identification demands a skill that may be termed as 'specialized skill' that needs training, know-how, aptitude, resource, personnel, time, etc., to prepare such feasibility reports: and

(vi) Some university/colleges/research organizations are found in recent times undertaking feasibility studies in developing countries and these studies would be enriched more if a scientific methodology is adopted in such studies.

5

The Historical Research Method

The term 'history' has been derived from 'Historia' , which means learning or acquiring knowledge through research. History is the record of past events. It is complete, accurate meaningful record of man's achievements. Allan Newins says that history is an integrated narration or description of past events or facts, written in spirit of critical inquiry to find out the whole truth. History helps us to study the society, its structure, functions and processes. A social scientist gets insight into the past through history. Past always contains elements of the present. Past, present and future are all well inter-linked. As pointed out by *Carter V. Goode* "History embraces the entire field of the human past and is as board as life itself. Our human past includes many areas of social experience and activities that frequently have proved more significant. The task of a historian is to collect information about the past events and to analyze them correctly. He is concerned with an accurate account of a particular happening, stressing the location and the date. That is, it works out "an accurate record of how, when and where the event started; how it progressed and how and when it ceased. The historian explains the event by describing the conditions which led unto it and out of which it grew."

The historical method consists of heuristic criticism, synthesis and exposition. Originally developed by the philologists during the age of Renaissance, when they laid down rules for the purpose of dealing with classical and sacred texts, the historical method was adopted by the Benedictines of France during the seventeenth century. Even today historical method has greater significance for social research. There are a number of social problems which are to be studied with historical background. Historical studies have made important contributions to various social science disciplines. In the field of economics, sociology, cooperation, politics, education and psychology, many studies are essentially historical in approach. For instance, History of Cooperative thought, History of Cooperative Development, Evaluation of Panchayati Raj System, Pattern of Leadership Development, History of Social Legislation, etc. In all these studies historical data have greater relevance.

Meaning of Historical Research

Historical Research has been defined by *Walter R. Borg* in the following words: "Historical research is the systematic and synthesis of objective location, evaluation, and synthesis of evidence in order to establish facts and draw conclusions concerning past events".

According to Shiek Ali "Historical research is digging into the past in order to re-enact the past in its entirety, to reconstruct the past event as fully as they must have happened, to explain the meaning and significance of those events, to correct the wrong notions so long prevalent, if any, and to elaborate, analyze, synthesize and philosophies the ideas in the light of the knowledge we possess."

Robert G. Murdick of Florida Atlantic University says the "Historical Research is concerned with establishing the occurrence of unique events. Although one phase of historical research consist only of determining past events, the ultimate phase deals with the interpretation of such events in the past and present, the establishment of pattern of relationship and the starting point of projecting trends." Historical research is essential for both basic and applied research in social sciences. The main aim of historical research, according to *Frederick Lamson Whitney*, is to apply the method of reflective thinking to social problems, still unsolved, by means of discovery of past trends of event, fact and attitude. It traces lines of development in human thought and action in order to reach some basis for social activity. *P.V. Young* describes historical method as the induction of principles through research into the past and social forces which have shaped the present. The explanations of the present derived from historical inquiries are sometimes called "genetic studies". Historical research like all other research is not just concerned with digging up facts. Evaluation and interpretation are integral parts of legitimate research. The historical researcher must concern himself with critical evaluation of source documents in terms of authority, content and meaning and interpretation of records in terms of general laws, trends or hypothesis.

Sources of Historical Research

The major sources of historical data are as follows:

1. Printed books, papers, literature and magazines
2. Documents
3. Remains
4. Materials of cultural history and of analytical history
5. Diaries
6. Memoirs
7. Confessions
8. Autobiographies
9. Sacred achieves
10. Covert diplomatic agreements
11. Statistical materials
12. Suppressed inventions
13. Personal letters
14. Personal accounts

15. Personal sources of authentic observers and witnesses
16. Artistic materials, historical paintings, portraits, charts, maps etc.

As pointed out by *P.V. Young*, when, how and under what circumstances to use any or all of these sources depends to a great extent on the discretion of the researcher, his interest, the purpose and the scope of his study and the availability of these sources. It is always advisable for a historical researcher before consulting and drawing upon historical documents, to consult a historian and explain the purpose and the scope of his study and get his suggestions as to methods of gathering and interpreting these sources.

In historical research, if the approach is to be objective, it is essential that the data are reliable, relevant and adequate. It should also help effective evaluation of the past. *P.V. Young* says the historical data are reliable and adequate for social research: *(i)* when they are presented as complexes of social forces, *(ii)* when social phenomena meaning fully depict intricate social process, *(iii)* when sets of inter-relationships---psychological, economic, education, political, religious – contribute to a unified whole a configuration or complex pattern.

Evaluation of Historical Data

In historical research, related documents provide the sole source of information. The documents are "reports of events consisting of impressions made on some human brain by past events and consciously or deliberately recorded for the purpose of transmitting information. The evaluation of the documents is of crucial importance to enable the researcher to place each bit of information in its proper perspective and draw sound conclusions. The evaluation of historical evidence is usually known as 'Historical Criticism'. Historical Criticism is generally divided into two groups, namely: *(a)* External Criticism or Heuristics which means inciting to find out *(b)* Internal criticism or Hermeneutics or Interpretative Criticism. The main aim of these two types of criticism is to pronounce whether a given idea is acceptable as a fact or not. Events, occurrences and happenings as presented in the records may or not conform to reality, for they might have been distorted, twisted or misrepresented. Thus, through these methods the authenticity and creditability of the data are tested.

External Criticism (Heuristics)

This is concerned with the genuineness of the documented words. External criticism deals with data relating to form and appearance rather than meaning of contents. External criticism is sometimes called lower criticism because it is a preliminary or preparatory step providing the data to be used in the second phase known as internal criticism. In testing the genuineness of a document the problem of external criticism involves the question of authorship and his qualification as a reporter, factor or conditions that may have influenced the production of the document, such as time, place, purpose and circumstances of compositions and the extent of which the document reads true to the origin. In determining the truth and value of the document, the researcher has to see the question of authorship, his personality, character, position, general qualifications as a reporter, alertness, character bias special qualifications and or disqualifications as a reporter of the matter, interest in the events, his technical knowledge for learning and reporting the events, the method of writing document from memory, after consultation with others, the data and year of documentation and such other details.

Internal Criticism (Hermeneutics)

Internal criticism is nothing but evaluating the accuracy and value or worth of the statements within the document. In other words it is testing the creditability of the data. This process is also called higher criticism. A historical researcher must put his documentary evidence to the test of truthfulness as well as competence. *Carter V. Good* says that many authentic or genuine documents may not be completely accurate or truthful and require the process of internal criticism in the form of textual criticism as well as investigation of such factors as the competence, good faith, position and bias of the author of the document. Internal criticism involves a scientific examination of the relevance of the data, correction of errors and rejection of the information that is found wanting. Internal criticism is much more difficult than external criticism because it involves evaluating the writer, his bias and the possible motives for distortion. This evaluation requires wide knowledge, practical experience and training in psychology.

Internal criticism is of two types—negative criticism and positive criticism. Negative criticism is to examine the circumstances in which a person wrote the document, whether he was in a position to ascertain the truth and to reveal the real story and whether he was guided by motives or bias. Positive criticism seeks to find out whether the contents of the documents are true or otherwise. In historical research, both negative and positive criticisms are essential.

Conditions Necessary for Historical Research

Although the historical method appears to be simple in its application it is in a way much more complicated then some of the other methods. Historical method demands experience and competence. The following are the conditions necessary for historical research:

1. Selection of a topic for research—The researcher must be capable of choosing a suitable topic for his research. The subject selected may be related to a region, period, trend or a person.
2. The researcher must have a great deal of social insight and historical orientation. Mastery of sources is another requirement for a historical researcher. He must also have the capacity to digest and master materials.
3. The historical researcher must posses an imagination of the topic chosen for research.

4. The researcher must have knowledge of related social science. This would enable him to analyze the topic in its proper perspective.
5. A wide educational background is a must for an effective use of the historical method. This background would enable him to understand the topic in an inter-related manner.
6. The researcher must have familiarity with the general field of his topic and clarity regarding his own objectives. He must also have a thorough knowledge about the work already done in the field.
7. Historical research demands experience and competence not only in assembling data but also in relating them to the major influencing conditions and in assessing their significance in the particular context.
8. The researcher must have an objective approach in analysis. He must take both an analytical and synthetic view of the facts. He has to take an overall view to assess the true relationship between the events themselves and between the events and the environment.
9. The researcher must be in a position to know his own limitations in understanding and interpreting the events. This position would make him receptive to new ideas and knowledge put forth by more intelligent and experienced persons.
10. The researcher must be aware of the limitations in the historical sources that he uses in his study. This fact will induce him to probe further into the matter.
11. Availability of good library facilities.
12. Availability of adequate grants.
13. Favorable arrangements for work, with necessary tools such as computer services, calculating machines, artists to draw graphs, maps etc.

Steps Involved in Historical Research

The steps involved in historical research are discussed below:

Selection of the Problem

The first and foremost problem of a historical research is identification of an appropriate topic for study. It must be understood that all problems may not lend themselves for historical analysis. The selection of a suitable topic/ problem/area depends on the researcher's intellectual caliber, skill, aptitude, interest, training, courage, imagination and wide reading. The selection of a topic also depends on the availability of adequate time data and financial sources. The topic to be selected must be specific and not general in order to facilitate in-depth study. It must be practical or pragmatic. It must present an original contribution. The topic must have central or unifying theme, a direction by progression, continuity and the promise of yielding specific conclusions. Further, the researcher has to formulate the objectives of the study. Unless the objectives are specified with sufficient precision to ensure that the data collected are relevant to the question raised, the study may not provide the desired information.

Formulation of Hypothesis

The next step is formation of suitable hypothesis for the study. A hypothesis directs our search for the order among facts and suggest explanations for certain facts and guide in investigation. *Pauline V. Young* says that "Formulation of hypothesis gives definite point to the enquiry aids in establishing direction in which to proceed, and helps to delimit the field of enquiry by singling out the pertinent facts on which to concentrate and by determining which facts should be set aside and thus prevents a blind search and indiscriminate gathering of data which may later prove irrelevant to the problem under study.

Preparations for Collection of Data

The researcher must make necessary arrangements for collection of relevant and adequate data for his study. In the beginning he has to prepare an exhaustive bibliography on the subject and sketch out an outline. In historical research unlike other forms of research, the investigator must deal with data that is already in existence. Therefore, he must identify the sources of data. There are primary and secondary sources. While gathering data he must go through all the sources available and make a note of the related facts. Effective note-taking procedure is very important in historical research. Goode and Scates say that to make good progress in answering historical questions the researcher should collect the material systematically. For this purpose he needs a well-arranged plan of note-taking. It is also essential to keep the note-system flexible to enable to add additional materials without re-arranging the old material. Historical researcher should make three different kinds of notes. The first one is a bibliographical note in which the author, title, page, place, date of publication and other information about the document are noted. The second type is the subject note which contains the great body of notes. The third kind of note is usually referred to as the method notes which contain the suggestive and interpretative ideas. Separate cards or sheets of different colours may be used for note-taking various categories of materials and each card/sheet may be coded to indicate the hypothesis or sub-topic to which the note relates.

Evaluation of Data

The next step is criticism of data. This is nothing but testing and evaluating the authenticity and accuracy of data collected through primary and secondary sources. The evaluation of historical data is known as historical criticism. The data is verified and validated through the process of external criticism (i.e., question of authorship, time, place, genuineness and actual language or text of the original document) and the process of internal criticism (i.e., questions of accuracy and value of the statement made). Historical criticism is of fundamental importance in historical research, because writing of a correct historical account depends on the criticism of data collected.

Organization of Data

After the data has been evaluated, it is necessary to organize it into meaningful form. This process is called synthesis or grouping of facts. An effective synthesis calls for a thorough understanding of the meaning, implication of every piece of evidence, understanding the works that are related to the theme, critical thinking and ability to interpret and arrange the data. The data may be arranged on a thematic or topical basis with reference to the contents, on a chronological basis with reference to the period and date of happening and on a geographical basis with reference to places or to combine different processes. This arrangement is necessary not only to draw conclusions and to present them logically but to discard the irrelevant facts. This process of course requires sound thinking, wide reading, greater imagination and good training.

Interpretation and Writing Report

After the data has been arranged and systematized, the researcher must have a mental outline of his report. The outline serves as a working plan. It is the blue print of the entire research work. It helps the researcher to arrange his ideas effectively. The outline must be always flexible to enable the researcher to change when necessary. The researcher must also order the headings and sub-headings. All the facts must be grouped together under major and sub-headings. The division of headings must be according to a logical order. Weakness in the logical organization of a report of historical research suggests weakness in the researcher's understanding and analysis of the problem. *Carter V. Goode and Douglas E. Scates* say that "historical composition is a synthetic and constructive process that involves the mechanical problem of documentation, the logical problem of selection and arrangement of topics and sub-topics and the philosophical problem of interpretation."

Therefore they suggest that an appropriate combination of the chronological and topical plans for arrangement of topics and materials is recommended. The researcher should see that all facts are grouped properly. In writing the report, there must be an effective beginning and an appropriate finish for each of the passages that contain related ideas. The beginning must create the interest of the readers and lead to the development of logical ideas. The discussion must be critical and analytical. All statements must be supported by proper evidence drawn from the sources. The language and style are significant aspects of a report of historical research. A clear lucid style is imperative if communication between the researcher and the reader is to be established. It is always desirable to avoid emotional dramatization or exaggerated rhetoric. Illustrations and examples are most effective when they are based on common experiences. Abstract terminology must be avoided. As pointed out by *Franscesco Cordasco and Elliott Gatner* of Long Island University "every report must be attempted to solve some intellectual problem. No research paper is successful unless it contributes to the solution of a problem and adds to the knowledge of the research". It is essential that the report should show the essence of the historical investigation indicating the depth of the study.

Usefulness of Historical Research

Historical research is an attempt to make a diligent and systematic enquiry or investigation into a subject in order to discover facts and/or revise the known facts and/or put the facts into theories. Historical research is useful both for theoretical and practical purposes. It has made important contributions to various branches of social sciences. Historical method includes study of life histories, history of various organizations and institutions. Historical research enables us to get an accurate knowledge of the past. When we analyze the past and present, it is possible to predict the future. It helps in choosing suitable policy or action among a number of alternatives. Through historical study, it is possible to study the development of a particular idea, concept philosophy etc. It is also possible to make comparative studies for a historical period of time, factors, situations etc. In economics, comparative studies may be made in terms of growth, national product, savings, investment and trends in operation by evaluation. In business, study of history of individual companies would help us for interpretation of their impact on economy. Historical research enables communities to understand their relationship with the past and to plan more intelligently for the future. It gives people a sense of continuity and consciousness of unity in their effort and achievements. As pointed out by *Carter V. Goode,* in education to understand it as a social process with a long history, and also to evaluate school theories and plans, it is necessary to know the historical evidence. Similarly in educational sociology for studying certain problem areas, historical sources as well as approaches are frequently used. In psychology also, historical approach can make great contributions. For instance many genetic, clinical, case biographical, autobiographical studies are essentially historical in approach. In the field of cooperation, both for academic and practical purposes, many problems can be studied by historical approach. For example the Evaluation of Cooperative Doctrines, the History of Cooperative Development etc., need historical evidence for a deep study. In sociology, attempts are made to study social institutions such as caste system, marriage and cultural groups in historical background. As pointed out by P.V. Young, historians, philosophers, social psychiatrists, literary men, as well as social scientists, use the historical approach as an aid in visualizing society as a dynamic organism and its structures and functions as steadily growing and undergoing change and transformation.

6

Case Study

One of the simplest methods of social research is case study. By means of analyzing a case the researcher can study the entire life history of the unit. It goes deep into the problems and the interaction between factors is noted by measuring the intensity of influence by one variable over the other. *John Best* says that, "case study is concerned with everything that is significant in the history or development of the case. The purpose is to understand the life cycle or an important part of the life cycle of an individual unit. This unit may be a person, a family, a group, a social institution or an entire community. The case method probes deeply and intensively, analyses interaction between the factors that produce change or growth. It emphasizes the longitudinal or genetic approach showing development over a period of time."

Case study is very useful for business research. If we want to study the growth and development of a company it is an ideal method of research. Or if we want to study a particular problem of a company deeply, say labour unrest, absenteeism or industrial sickness, this method of research will help the researcher in many ways. It takes less time to collect data and less experience than other methods of research like survey. Any beginner of social research can attempt case study and then he can go for other methods of research.

Mr. Herbert Spencer, Mr. Frederick Le Play and Dr. William Healey were the pioneers of case study method. The French Social reformer Frederick Le Play's (1806-1882) study on the standard of living of families was kind of case-study. *Dr. William Healey,* another pioneer of the case study used this method to study juvenile delinquency covering a large number of cases, i.e., constituting the juvenile delinquents as the population of the study.

A case study is deep and intensive study of a particular social unit. It also a diagnostic study oriented towards finding out what is happening and why it happening and what can be done about it. Some experts refer to it as insight—stimulating study. It is also known as historical genetic method and holistic approach. A case study covers all aspects of social unit. It also seeks to determine social process; it reveals the complexity of factors and indicates their sequences and inter-relationships. Case study, says Cahrles H. Cooley "deepens our perception and gives us a clearer insight into life." According to *Pauline V. Young;* "Case study is a method of exploring and analyzing the life of social unit—be that unit a person, a family, institution, cultural group or even entire community." *Mr. William J. Goode and Mr. Paul K. Hatt* wrote that "case study is a way of organizing social data so as to preserve the unitary character of the social object being studied." According to F.L. Whitney, "case study is a complete analysis and report of the status of an individual subject with respect as a rule to specific phases of his total personality." Mr. James A. Black and Mr. Dean J. Champion wrote that case studies were usually characterized as thorough examination of specific social settings or particular aspects of social settings, including in varying details psychological descriptions of persons in those settings."

Significance of Case study

1. Case study helps in formulating valid hypothesis. Study of relevant literature and case study are the two potent sources of hypothesis.
2. It helps in framing questionnaire or schedule. By knowing the characteristics of individual units we can prepare the tools in a right way.
3. It aids in sampling. By studying individual units thoroughly the researcher can put them in definite class or type and it helps in perfect classification of the sample.
4. It locates deviant cases. Deviant cases are those units which go against a hypothesis.
5. Case study enlarges the range of personal experience of the researcher. Under case study the whole range of subject's life is studied and the range of knowledge is enlarged. With this gain the researcher gets an intimate knowledge of many aspects of the unit.
6. As case study covers the entire life of the unit, it is inclusive and intensive in nature. Hence, there is a possibility of studying various aspects of a problem.

Characteristics of Case Study

The characteristics of the case study method are as follows:

1. Case study is a deep, detailed and intensive study of a social unit.
2. It is a comprehensive study.
3. It is a method of qualitative analysis.
4. In case study, all the variables and traits are linked with one another.
5. It is a flexible method.
6. In case study there are chances for wide variety of units to be selected.
7. It preserves wholeness of the units, i.e., it is an approach which views any social unit as a whole.

8. In case study the complex factors are studied; and finally
9. Traits are the subject matter of the study.

Precautions Essential in Choosing an Object of Case Study

A case refers to a unit of study. The unit may be a person, a family or a social group, a class of persons, a set of relationship or processes such as family crisis, friendship formation and cultural groups. The following are the precautions which are essential in choosing an object of case study.

1. Selection of typical and representative unit.
2. Identification of situations and problems.
3. Time to be covered—the phase of life cycle.
4. Unitary character of the unit—breadth of data, levels of data, use of indices and types.
5. Quantity of data.
6. Availability of data and its reliability.
7. Cost to be incurred.
8. Time to be spent.
9. Researcher's courage, interest, skill and training in research.
10. Possibility to repeat case study.

If these precautions are carefully adhered to by the researcher, the case study will be valid and useful.

Sources of Data

In case study the information may be collected from varied sources such as:

1. Life histories
2. Personal records
3. Personal documents
4. Personal letters

5. Confessions
6. Biographies
7. Interviewing individuals
8. Observations.

Case studies are not limited to any single source of data collection. They employ a number of sources. *Mr. Thomas and Znaniecki* made extensive use of "life reaching the actual experiences and attitudes of person, and groups as well as in securing a cross section of the entire process of their social, becoming". Many other have made case studies with interviews, conferences at specified intervals, conversations, observations, post-experimental interviews, experimental studies etc. Sometimes the researcher has to use different aspects of the cases. Thus, to collect reliable and accurate data the researcher has to employ various sources and techniques in case studies.

Steps Involved in Case Study

The various steps involved in any case study are as follows:

Selection of Cases and Identification of Situation

The researcher has to decide, which unit has to be taken up for study? What aspect or what period of life of unit can be studied? What are the situations in which unit exists? All these questions should be answered first. The researcher therefore, has to choose representative and typical units. The selection of such units of course depends on the ability and skill of the researcher.

Gathering and Recording of Data

While gathering data, the researcher has to keep in mind the continuity, breadth and level of data to preserve the completeness and validity of data, a broad array of facts have to be collected. Therefore, it is pertinent that the researcher should use different techniques and tools to collect data about the different aspects of the unit. Study of personal documents, life histories, observations, interviews, questionnaires, schedules, a variety of tests like intelligent test, achievement tests, aptitude tests are certain techniques adopted in case study for gathering data. Again the data should be recorded uniformly, topic wise, accurately and objectively with clarity, under principal themes of investigation. The data should be complete and up to date and of easy reference. Again the careful collection and recording of data depends on the skill and the ability of the researcher. He should keep an alert mind and try to seek more information and derive special features from them.

Interpretation and Reporting of Data

Interpretation is an objective judgment based on background knowledge of a situation-appraisal of an event. It is the search for the broader meaning of the research findings. It is the deeper sense of the investigation. It places a particular event in the larger flow of events. It is the colour, the atmosphere, the human element that gives meaning to a fact. It is in short setting sequence and about all significance. The facts collected must be clarified, explained and interpreted. The interpretation must be in logical and convenient form. Qualitative classification and building up a proper background theory are also very essential. Good interpretation depends on the researcher's knowledge, imagination and wisdom.

The findings have to be adequately reported in order to make it more valuable to the public. Reporting the research findings to the public is thus an important part of any type of social investigation. The main aim of reporting is to present the results of the investigation in lucid and plain language. The researcher has to present the problem investigated, the research techniques and methods employed, the result and conclusions arrived at as a result of the investigation. The report must be in such a manner that the reader can easily understand, assess and enable him to verify the validity of the conclusions, in short, the report must have unity, clarity, readability and accuracy.

Usefulness of Case Study

As case study is a deep and diagnostic study, it has been praised as a useful research technique. Goode and Hatt say that "as against the analysis of individual traits alone, it is a highly fruitful approach as yet insufficiently exploited by those who are currently doing research into research techniques". The case study method has been very useful to social science research in many ways. Several social scientists have assessed the importance of the case data to social research. *P.V. Young* says that "Case data are vivid, absorbing and tend to reproduce a person's social attitudes and values." Social scientists like *Thomas and Znaniecki* maintain that case data constitute "the perfect type of sociological material as they represent a more enlightening and fundamentally more real record of personal experiences with a wealth of concrete detail, vivid memories, tension situations and which shape the attention of most skilled investigators using other techniques". The following are some of the specific advantages of the case study.

1. Case study helps to probe the entire life span of a social unit intensively and to analyze the complex factors that are influencing the social unit. It indicates their sequences and inter-relationships. It also covers a wide range of information about the cases. Thus, it gives a greater depth of knowledge and experience which may be of great use for further research.
2. Case data are vivid, absorbing and tend to reproduce a person's social attitudes and values.
3. Case study facilitates to understand everything about a social unit and the variety of habits, traits and qualities combined in a social unit.
4. Case study helps to secure detailed information about the growth of the unit, group structure, individual life pattern etc.
5. The relationship between individual and society is well brought out in the case study.
6. Its techniques are often used in pure research, sociology and economics with a view to develop

certain theories and broad principles.

7. Case studies are indispensable for the research and administrative purposes.
8. It is also easy to generalize cases with case study and helps to prepare a plan of action for treatment.
9. Case study is followed for comparison, classification, analysis and for the formulation of hypothesis leading to further research.
10. Case studies also help the researchers to frame schedule and questionnaires.
11. Case data are useful to pure research in furnishing clues for further research.
12. They are also useful for diagnosis and other practical case by case problems.

Limitations of Case Study

Though case study method has contributed much to the social research, some social scientists have raised some objections against the value and validity of case studies. Following are some of the limitations commonly attributed to case studies.

1. Case study does not provide universal, impersonal, and common aspects of a phenomenon.
2. There is a tendency for a researcher to draw generalization after studying a few cases, which may not be relevant to all situations.
3. There is a tendency to over emphasis the unique or unusual events which are seldom comparable.
4. The subjective data collected do not lend themselves to quantitative check.
5. It is costly, time consuming and wasteful in certain cases where the objectives are limited.
6. It is generally viewed that case study is loose and unsystematic and the generalization drawn from a few cases are not always accurate.

7. In the case study method, there is a temptation to ignore the basic principles of Research Design.

But most of the problems can be avoided through improved techniques of case studies. Social scientists like *Carl Rogers, Elton Mayo, Mirra Komarovsky* and *Alfred Kinsey* have used the new techniques of collecting, recording and processing case data. And thus, they have made case study as one of the important methods of social research.

7

Survey Method

Social Surveys—A Review

Social surveys, says *P.V. Young* in her book "Scientific Social Surveys and Research," are as old as the history itself. The ever growing socio-economic and other problems in the human society stimulated the social scientists to engage the study of those problems and to find out the causes and to take remedial measures. Several economists, sociologists, anthropologists, social reformers and social scientist have conducted a number of different types of surveys either independently or in collaboration with Government or research institutions. Those include, general specific and census surveys. The social scientists thus attempted to use social survey technique to gather facts in a systematic manner right from the earlier periods.

Early Surveys

P.V. Young writes in the above noted book that Herodotus had recorded about a survey of population and wealth in Egypt in 300 B.C. A reference was found about the ideas of social investigation in the Doomsday Book of William the Conqueror in the eleventh century. According to *Mark*

Abrams the social surveys of today have their methodological roots in the enquiries carried out by three men namely Charles Booth, B. Seebohm Rowntree and Professor Arthur Bowley. But one of the earliest attempts was made by John Howard, a famous English philanthropist and prison reformer in the second half of the 18th century. He studied the conditions of prison and prisoners. He also employed a variety of techniques to gather a specific body of facts. Another pioneer in this field was the French social reformer by name Frederic Le Play, who in the middle of the 19th century methodically studied 1000 working class family budgets. He was the first to use inter-disciplinary approach in social surveys. He gathered the facts through personal interviews and observation. The English reformer and statistician Mr. Cherles Booth conducted a survey in 1886 on poverty of labourers in the East side of London. This was also a pioneering work in social surveys. His survey includes the aspects like income, hours and conditions of work, housing, standards of living, number of children, size of household in relation to size and type of dwelling, type and frequency of sickness, leisure activities, and club and union membership. In 1899, B.S. Rowntree made a study of the city of New York and again in 1939 to evaluate the changes in the standard of living of the people. Thus, he first introduced the method of comparative study in social survey. He obtained the required facts directly from the working class families by using interviewers. His most important contribution was that he gave far greater precision to the concept of poverty. He was the first sociologist to draw attention to the cyclical pattern of poverty. Mr. Rowntree's approach thus varied in methodological aspects from that of Mr. Booth. His study was published under the title 'Poverty: A study of Town Life'. Yet another important social survey was initiated by Prof. Arthur Bowley, a famous statistician in 1912. He studied the working class conditions in reading, for the first time through random sampling technique. Bowley's important methodological contribution was his application of the principles of random sampling, which came to act as decisive stimulus to social surveys. Later in almost all the poverty surveys the same method was used. Professor Bowley had also introduced comparative studies and varied methods of investigation in social surveys. In 1928, Ford undertook a study in Southampton following the methods of Professor Bowley and the same was published under the title "Work and Wealth in a Modern Port". Again in 1928, Sir Hubert Llewelyn Smith one of the associates of Booth conducted a study on the changes in the working of socio-economic life of London labourers. He illustrated the results through charts, maps etc. In 1935, Rowntree initiated a second survey in New York and again a follow-up survey in 1950 in the same place in collaboration with G.R. Lavers. The findings were published under the title "Poverty and Welfare state". This study received greater public attention at that time. In the middle of thirties, survey activity began to receive greater importance in many fields. The establishment of the Government Social Survey in 1941 was one of the noted developments in the field of social survey in Great Britain. This organization initiated a number of studies in the field of town planning, housing, sickness, consumption expenditure, national income, nutrition, health, industry, mining, education, employment, colonial affairs and industrial research on noise, light, heating in domestic dwellings, on road traffic problems etc. Further, opinion, market, population, urban life, rural life, audience, traveling, family expenditure, social mobility, political behaviour, old age, juvenile delinquency, industrial relations and moral surveys were initiated at different places in Great Britain by the individual social scientists, the Government and the research organizations. It must be also noted that several independent research establishments emerged which as commercial bodies, have specialized in the planning and execution of social surveys on behalf of Government or of any one who liked to use survey method in tackling problems. The work of these specialized research bodies played a significant part in social research in Great Britain.

As in England, in the USA, several socio-economic surveys were initiated by the social scientists since 1890. The first study of those kinds giving an account of tenement conditions in New York with clear explanations appeared in the year 1890. The next important social inquiry into housing conditions of the State was conducted by the New York Tenement House Commission in 1900. Similarly, the slum conditions were surveyed in 1902. Another important study under the title, "The jungle describing the working conditions of the meat-packing labourers, exploitation by the industrial monster" was published in 1906. This study was very helpful for enacting the first social legislation namely "Pure Food and Drug Act". In 1907 the Russel Sage Foundation was established with a view to improving the social and living conditions in the USA, and separate department of surveys was created by the Foundation in 1912. This was another development in the history of survey movement in the USA. In 1909, the Pittsburg Survey— "A study of the Effects of Urbanization" was initiated by Paul Kellogg with the help of trained social economists and professional social workers. A noted feature of this survey was the introduction of the inter-disciplinary approach to study the effects of urbanization. This was an elaborate and a systematic study whose findings were published in six volumes. Later, on the advice of the Russel Sage Foundation, a series of small studies related to social problems were undertaken in a number of communities. In 1914, the Springfield Survey— "A Study of Social Conditions of an American Small City" was undertaken by Shelby Harrison of Illinois State. This enquiry touched the primary aspects of the city life and analyzed the important social problems. For the successful completion of the survey, Shelby Harrison, not only enlisted the support of different agencies and individuals but employed publicity campaign before his field work, to mobilize interest and secure cooperation from the people. He also used exhibits to explain the city's problems.

In 1935, Sir John Boyd Orr, undertook the first modern systematic examination of consumption and standard of living of people. In 1938, Alfred C. Kinsey and his associates conducted a survey on the sexual behaviour of Americans. The chief objectives were to collect sufficient information's to describe American sexual behaviour and to establish that factors account for individual differences in sexual behaviour and for group differences among the various major segments of the population. This study covered a sample of 5300 persons. The Survey Division of the Office of War Information of the U.S. Government in 1943 initiated a survey to establish certain facts about the nature and extent of industrial absenteeism in war industry and to determine some of the factors leading to such absence. This survey covered a sample of 1800 respondents, representing 100 workers systematically from 18 different plants. Further, a survey on prejudice and personality was made in 1944. The National Association of Broadcasters commissioned a national survey on the understanding the acceptance of radio by the public in 1945. The main object was to assess the strength and weakness of the radio industry to ascertain where radio stands with the public, in order to blue print a sound plan of action for the future of broadcasting. The sampling size of the survey was 2500. In 1946, "An Enquiry into the thinking of Americans about the Atomic Bomb and International Affairs", was planned by the Committee on Social Science Research Council and conducted by the American Institute of Public Opinion. A sample of 3000 persons was covered under this study.

The surveys conducted earlier thus stimulated the American social scientists to recognize the survey as a realistic and scientific method of studying the characteristics of the American life. Later a number of individual, regional and national surveys were conducted in different parts of the country. The growth of private and government research bodies was another noted development in the survey research. The individual researchers as well as research establishments studied systematically the problem of social security, economic conditions, employment and unemployment, wages, health, housing, child welfare services, crime and delinquency. Individual researchers, colleges and universities began to use survey research as an important method in all social science disciplines. Today the social survey plays a significant role in the formulation of national policy and it is recognized that social surveys are indispensable for mobilizing the forces of community in tackling social problems.

The review of social surveys initiated in Great Britain and the USA revealed that the social scientists had used improved devices and techniques for the selection of samples, obtaining information from the respondents and for analysis of data. They had employed particularly random sampling and systematic sampling techniques, machine tabulation, statistical analysis, comparisons, participant observation, personal interview and used secondary data as well as the well prepared and pre-tested schedules.

Social Survey in India

Research studies based on survey method were increasingly undertaken in a number of developed, under developed, less developed and developing countries. For instance, in India a number of socio-economic surveys were initiated right from the end of the 18th century. Several economic problems were systematically studied by individual, institutions, the Government and the Reserve Bank of India. The important earliest surveys were: *(i)* A sociological and statistical survey of some Madras villages by Sir Theodore Morison in 1931; *(ii)* Socio-economic survey of Madras and Bombay provinces by Dr. Gilbert Slater and Dr. Mann in 1918. In all these surveys, the schedule and interview techniques were chiefly used to obtain accurate data. In 1921, a systematic and detailed investigation into the supply of milk in Lahore was undertaken. To assess the economic changes in the villages, the Royal Commission on Indian Agriculture stressed the importance of surveys in 1928. Professor S. Kesava Iyengar, conducted an economic survey in Hyderabad in 1929. This survey covered a sample of 4 districts and 12 villages. Personal interview techniques were chiefly employed. Data was also collected from the records of the village office. In 1936-37, Professor P.J. Thomas undertook a socio-economic survey in Madras state. This survey used improved techniques of investigation and statistical analysis. In the following year (1937-38) another urban survey was taken up by Professor Dr. Gadgil in Poona.

Prior to Independence, the survey studies initiated in

the country were limited and in most of the studies advanced research techniques were not employed. After independence, that too during the planning era survey research began to receive greater importance. A number of research bodies and institutions were set up. They have contributed much to the development of social surveys in the country. The Gokhale Institute of Politics and Economics and the Indian Statistical Institute had been conducting a number of enquiries on socio-economic problems of the society. For example, the Gokhale Institute of Politics and Economics engaged in a large number of studies between 1945 and 1952. The important studies conducted by the Indian Statistical Institute were survey related to consumer preference in Calcutta, Bengal Handloom survey, the survey of Rural Indebtedness, Agricultural Labour and the National Sample Survey. The National Sample Survey was started in 1950, which is conducting the biggest sampling survey in India. Another outstanding survey conducted in the country was the RBI's All India Rural Credit Survey headed by A.D. Gorwala in 1951. This was an economic survey aimed at the study of the patterns of agricultural credit in different parts of the country. This survey covered a sample of 1,27,343 families in 600 villages, selected in 75 districts all over the country. The random sampling technique was used for the selection of the units of study. Techniques like interviews, case studies and tools like schedules, questionnaires and records of different types were used in this study. This was one of the extensive studies, which provided innumerable statistical data relating to the agricultural credit. A survey on the levels of living in India was initiated by B.N. Ganguly and D.B. Gupta in 1954. This survey included 15 major States in the country. This study covered various aspects like economic, social, nutrition, housing, medical care, education, clothing, leisure, security, environment and consumption pattern.

An outstanding development in the country was the setting up the National Council of Applied Economic Research at New Delhi which is an important research body in the country. The NCAER has initiated a series of national and regional studies covering several facts of human life.

Some of the important socio-economic surveys were: *(i)* The Urban Savings Survey in Delhi(1959); *(ii)* The All India Saving Survey in (1960); *(iii)* The Attitudes Towards and Motivation for Savings (1963); *(iv)* A study on Contractual Saving in Urban India (1963); *(v)* The All India Household Survey of Income, Saving and Consumption Expenditure (1972). In all these surveys improved research techniques were employed. The sample, random sampling, stratified random sampling and probability sampling techniques and tools like schedules, questionnaires etc. were used. Statistical analysis and comparisons were also made. Besides these surveys, the NCAER has conducted some techno-economic surveys. The Techno-Economic Survey of West Bengal (1959-60), Gujarat (1959) and U.P. (1962) were some of the important such surveys conducted at the requests of the Governments concerned.

The RBI conducted the All India Debt and Investment Survey in 1961-62 and 1971-72. The former one was conducted to estimate the debt, investment and other related characteristics of rural households not only for the country as a whole but also for major individual states. The second All India Debt and Investment Survey was a countrywide investigation on household indebtedness and investments. This survey was confined to the entire rural and urban areas of the country. A two stage stratified random sample design with villages as first stage unit, and household as second stage unit was adopted for the survey. The total sample size was 12,452. Schedules were chiefly used to obtain data from the households.

Survey method is exhaustive in nature and covers wider population and geographical area. It has immense use for a social researcher and is a method of research widely used by social researchers. It is a process under which data are collected systematically from the population or a section of the population. For a social researcher, the use of survey research has abundant value and is a popular method of research that is often used.

Definition

A survey is defined by experts as follows: Carter Goode defined it as, "a cooperative study of a current social problem, situation or population within definite geographical limits, ordinarily with some concern for a constructive programme of social reform and amelioration" C.A. Moser, an authority on Survey Research states that, "essentially social survey has become aware of a social problem, the relevant facts as to the dimensions and origins of the problems are collected by interviewing the people involved in the problem."

Wells defines survey as "a fact finding study dealing chiefly with working class poverty and with the nature and problems of the community."

P.V. Young—"In search of information which could be obtained easily from large, representative but diverse and widely scattered group of population, researchers have resorted to the sample surveys."

Features of Surveys

Surveys Collect Primary Information

Information or data needed for a survey research or problem are collected mainly through primary information. Collecting information at the very source is the basic strength of a survey. By means of selecting a sample, respondents are interviewed using tools like a schedule. Information are also collected through mailed questionnaire. Other techniques like observation is also used to collect primary information.

Surveys Vary in their Scope, Objective, Content and Approach

As different types of surveys are conducted to study different socio-economic problems, they vary in their scope, objective, content and approach. Moser and Kalton say that, "the coverage of a survey can range from a few case studies to a complete enumeration, from carefully selected samples to an arbitrary collection of volunteers."

Wider Coverage

Surveys cover a wider area. Universal problems like poverty, unemployment, etc. could be studied covering wider population. Any length or breadth of a country can be covered by surveys. Surveys conducted by world bodies like UNO, FAO, UNESCO cover many countries.

Problems of Deeper Nature

Acute social, economic, educational or administrative problems could be studied deeply applying survey method. Current problem which need immediate solution could also be dealt with surveys.

Entire Life of a Problem studied

The genesis of a problem from the inception is studied in a survey. Dimension of a problem is studied from various angles so as to pinpoint the real force behind a problem.

Survey is a Continuous Process

Surveys are conducted continuously focusing on a particular problem. Problem of long standing nature like unemployment need continuous study and monitoring. We have permanent bodies like National Sample Survey organization to provide information on various national issues.

Use of Sampling

This is the most distinctive nature of a survey. Hence, surveys are usually called as 'Sample Surveys'. Using the representatives of the population to collect data is a significant nature of a survey.

Pre-Test and Pilot study

Before a tool is used it is pre-tested in a survey. Likewise pilot study, which is a miniature study is conducted to find out the course of the main study.

Purpose of Surveys

According to Moser and Kalton, the expert team on social surveys, the purpose of surveys is as follows:

(a) The purpose of surveys is to provide someone with information. Here the researcher needs the aid of surveys to get information on varied aspects.

(b) "To a social scientist, a survey may equally have a purely descriptive purpose, as a way of studying social conditions, relationships and behaviour. The sort of information needed may be how families of different size, composition and social status spend their incomes, how people are reacting to the latest productivity drive, what relationship there appears to be between education and the possibility of moving up the social ladder."

(c) "Surveys have their usefulness both in leading to the formulation of hypotheses and at a more advanced stage, in putting them to the test. Their function in given research depends on how much is already known about the subject and on the purpose for which the information is required."

Subject Matter of Surveys

According to Moser and Kalton surveys have four types of subject matter. They are as follows:

The Democratic Characteristics of a Set of People

They are concerned with matters such as family or household composition, marital status, fertility, age and so on. These are certainly useful for social research as they mainly deal with human behaviour.

Their Social Environment

Their social environment is taken to cover all the social and economic factors to which people are subject, including occupation and income as well as housing conditions and social amenities. These are subjects which cover, in the widest sense, the question "How do people live?" Surveys on these conditions are essential for social research to find out the standard of living of the population and their purchasing power.

Their Activities

"By this is not meant occupation (which forms part of social environment) but, for instance, use of leisure, traveling habits, expenditure pattern, television viewing, radio-listening and newspaper reading. Much of the work of the government social survey lies in this field, and so does a good deal of social research." This approach of survey has enormous use for social research.

Their Opinions and Attitudes

"Opinion polls as the name suggests deal mainly with these, in many other surveys they are of marginal importance," For social research measurement of opinions and attitudes is necessary to know the tastes of the consumers, their liking for a product, size colour, and packing of a product. To improve the quality of a product and to introduce a new product opinions of consumers' must be necessary. Sometimes, even consumers may suggest a new product or would like to give a new brand name.

Advantage of Surveys

James Black and Dean Champion (Methods and Issues in Social Research) point out the following advantages of surveys:

1. Accumulation of information from individuals at relatively low cost to the researcher—surveys, particularly one using mailed questionnaire are cheaper means of collecting information. Information can also be collected from a large number of respondents.
2. Because large numbers of persons are usually included in a survey, generalization to larger population is more legitimate—opinion surveys conducted on a smaller scale reflect the general trends

of the population. Election predictions conducted on sample very many times prove to be accurate.

3. Surveys are flexible to permit the use of a variety of data collection techniques—observations, interviewing and questionnaires/schedules can be used in surveys to collect information from respondents.
4. Surveys sensitize the researcher to potential problems that were originally unanticipated or unknown—Surveys requesting written responses or verbal reactions from respondents often uncover facts previously unknown to the researcher.
5. Surveys are useful tools that enable investigators to verify theories—survey is one of the ways of obtaining support or lack of support for particular theoretical notions about people.

Other Advantages of Survey are Discussed Below

Moser and Kalton point out the purpose of surveys as, "a survey may be occasioned simply by a need for administrative facts on some aspects of public life; or be designed to investigate a cause–effect relationship or to throw fresh light on some aspect of sociological theory."

1. Its main purpose is to provide someone with information. It may be an individual researcher, an institution or even Government. They need information to implement new schemes. "To a social scientist, a survey may equally have a purely descriptive purpose, as a way of studying social conditions, relationships and behaviour."
2. It is to explain the relationship between a numbers of variables. Any problem will have the influence of variables, independent variables or dependent variable which have more influence over the other or over the problem could be clearly found out in a survey.
3. To make policies—Government and institutions need

lot of information to frame policies. Surveys are useful in such contexts.

4. Finding solutions to problems—Any research study is geared to find solutions to problems. Surveys are very purposeful in finding solutions to problem.
5. To evaluate programmes—when huge money is spent by Government or institution on various projects it is necessary to evaluate such programmes. Through such evaluations we can come to know the success or failure of such programmes. Community development schemes, family planning programmes are such examples.
6. To assess the benefits from a project—when projects or schemes are introduced it is necessary to know whether the project benefits have reached the people to whom it was intended. The type of benefits and the degree of benefits can also be measured by surveys.
7. To study problems—every problem in the working of an institution could be studied.
8. Consumer surveys—Through consumer surveys we can know the opinions and attitudes of consumers. Their reactions to new products, their quality and price could be measured. The strength and weaknesses of the competitors can also be measured by surveys.

Kinds of surveys

1. General or specific surveys—collecting general information about any population without any specific objective is called as general survey. If it is collected for specific purpose, then it becomes a specific survey.
2. Regular and ad-hoc surveys—when surveys are conducted at regular intervals it is called as Regular survey. Surveys on price level form part of such

surveys. Ad-hoc surveys are conducted to supplement missing information.

3. Preliminary and final surveys—pilot study is equal to that of a preliminary survey. Final survey is undertaken after the pilot study.
4. Census and sample surveys—under census survey entire population is covered and contacted to collect information. In sample surveys only a small part is taken as representative of the whole.
5. Social surveys—social surveys deal with current social problems of the society. Surveys on poverty, unemployment, housing, etc, form part of such surveys.
6. School surveys—Through school surveys, problems of education are studied.
7. Public opinion surveys—very often public opinion surveys are conducted to know the opinion of the population on certain issues or problems. Before elections, such surveys are conducted to know the party preference of voters.
8. Market surveys—such surveys are undertaken by industries and business community. When a new product is introduced the liking for such product, market share for such product, type of competition, etc. could be analyzed by market surveys.
9. Community surveys—For the development of a community such surveys are conducted. It helps the planning of schemes and the future development.
10. Observational surveys—It is to observe 'what people do?'

Steps in Conducting Surveys

Initial Preparation

Initial preparation is relating to the coverage of population, type of information to be collected, how to collect data? etc. Time and cost involved must also be planned.

Objectives and Resources

The objectives of the survey must be clearly laid down. According to Moser and Kalton, "It is not enough to say that the survey is intended to find out about the living conditions of old people; one should define exactly what for the purpose of the survey, is meant by an old person; whether the enquiry is to serve as a basis for inferences to a particular population of old people and if so, what their population is. One should make clear whether living condition's simply means a description of type of house, number of rooms, furniture and so forth, or whether income and expenditure data are wanted in order to gauge hardship. The initial statement should explain why the survey is being done, exactly what questions it means to cover, and what kind of results are expected. Most important, especially if the survey is being done for a client, the statement needs to discuss how the information is to be used and what degree of accuracy is required."

Coverage

Coverage denotes the coverage of population to be studied. Hence, the population must be defined in terms of its geographical, demographic and other boundaries. This must be decided properly in order to decide the size and type of sampling.

Collection of Data

The researcher must also decide the tools to be used to collect data. Mailed questionnaire, interview and observation are the important tools used in survey to collect data. While questionnaire is used it must be pre-tested and training for the interviewer must be given if it is administered through interview.

Processing of Data

Equal care must be shown for processing the data. The questionnaire must be scrutinized for errors, omission and overlapping before ready for tabulation. The type of statistical tool used must also be decided.

Report

The report must be written by the researcher himself. Viewing the topic and objectives of the study, the report must be schemed.

Limitations of Surveys

James Black and Dean Champion point out the following limitations of surveys:

1. Surveys are superficial reflections of population sentiments. As opinions of sample respondents are not deep they seldom represent the sentiments of the population.
2. Surveys, particularly political surveys, are unstable collections of population characteristics. "A study of opinion of a sample of individuals one week may be quite different from a similar survey of the same individuals a week or two late."
3. The researcher has little or no control over individual responses—"Those responding differ from those who do not respond. The potential bias resulting from such surveys significantly limits the generalization of one's findings to total population from which the original samples were obtained."
4. Statements about population from which samples are obtained are tentative—"The researcher manipulates the data obtained by tabular and statistical analyses and arrives at tentative conclusions related to some notions held about the targets population." Such conclusions may not represent the views of entire population.

8

Experimental Research

Experimental research has ample use in physical science researchers and it has limited use in marketing or social science research. It is a method of research where two groups are selected and compared. These comparisons may be relating to their behaviour, expression, feeling or emotions. Theses two groups are called as "Control group" and "Experimental group." Control group is an element not exposed to an experiment. Its behaviour is natural. On the other hand an experimental group is one that is exposed to an experimental variable. Individual could be changed from control group to experimental group in order to find out the changes in behaviour of the individual under both circumstances. In physical or chemical science substances or agents are changed.

Experimental research is defined by Black and Champion as, "all such designs that seek to control conditions within which persons are observed and analyzed may be called experimental designs."

Lack and others have defined experimental research as, "the actual trial of a proposed course of action or other hypotheses under consideration, so conducted that its effects can be observed (measured) objectively and distinguished from the effects of extraneous variables. When the effects on the pay off can be reliably isolated, the experimental design can be applied."

A term that is very often used here is the 'variable'. Variable is a factor or phenomenon which can influence change. Variables are classified into two namely dependent variables and independent variables. Independent variables will influence changes over the other whereas dependent variables would be influenced by independent variables. Variables are tested in control and experimental conditions. The influences of the variables could be measured by statistical tools in social research.

Preparations in Experimental Research

Luck and others suggest the following preparations in experimental research:

1. Determining the number and identifying the variables to be tested. The answers to this basic determination may not be at all evident and may require a very good preliminary study.
2. Selecting the range of values within which these variables would occur and being sensitive to the supposed casual factors. It would be sheer waste to exert or measure factors within ranges that would provide no information towards the problem solution.
3. Determining the character and inter-relations of the data and their method of measurement, which tend to be even more crucial than determination of the experimental techniques? Time and effort in planning should be carefully gauged to put due emphasis on the decision.
4. Determining the point at which internal validity may be increased only at the cost of lower external validity. In seeking to gain the former, the experimental model may become too unlike the real world or the subjects in the test may become biased, which would spoil the external validity. A proper

balance between theses qualities may be a nice question.

Types of Experimental Research

There are three major types of experimental designs namely:

1. Classical experimental design
2. After-only experimental design
3. Before-after experimental design

Classical Experimental Design

Goode and Hatt have explained this method intensively. They define it giving an example: "If there are two are more cases, and in one of them observation Z can be made, while in the other it cannot; and if factor C occurs when observation Z is made, and does not occur when observation Z is not made: then it can be asserted that there is a casual relationship between C and Z."

So in classical design two series of observations and situations are necessary. This type of research has greater use in biological or medical experiments. In marketing pharmaceutical goods, this research method may be helpful for a marketing research.

The above authors have explained this method by quoting an example of malaria infection and application for Atabrine to it, Atabrine is administered to one group, the experimental group and withheld from the other, the control group. If the experimental group recovers and the control group not, the conclusion is that Atrbrine and malaria systems are related. If all recover in both groups, then it can be concluded that Atabrine does not affect malaria.

After Only Experimental Design

This method assumes that prior to the introduction of the experimental factor, the control and experimental groups were identical and the nature is same. *Goode and Hatt* explained this as follows:

	Before	*After*	*Comparison:*
Experimental Group	X	X′	Before Vs After Difference = X1 - X
Control Group	X′	X1′	Difference = X1′ – X′

Before-After Experimental Research

In this method, the group is observed prior to its exposure to the experimental variable. That means to have a preliminary observational period so as to measure control behaviour and introduce a 'stimulus'. This is explained by Goode and Hatt as follows:

Experimental Group | Measurement Before Stimulus | Measurement After Stimulus

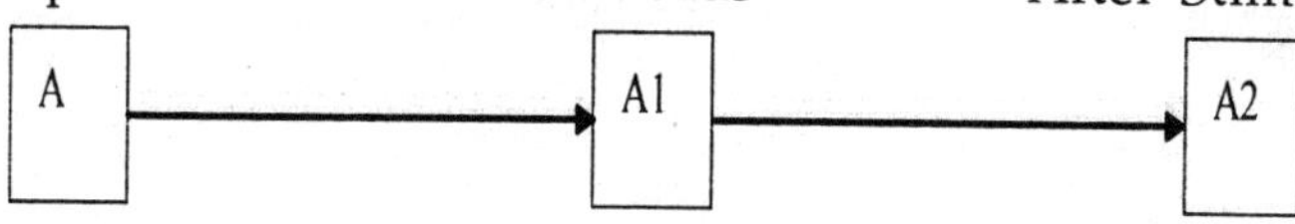

By means of using stimulus we can study the effect of previously identified experimental stimulus on experimental group and the effect of lack of stimulus on the control group.

SECTION – III

SELECTION OF RESEARCH PROBLEM

9

Selection of Research Problem

Socio-economic life in modern times is beset with innumerable problems. The immediate environment of the researcher provides ample scope for identification of a research problem. The recognition of and/or the existence of unsolved difficulties is the first symptom for locating a research problem. Coupled with this the felt need, constructive imagination and reflective thinking are the essential pre-requisites for identification of a research problem. The problem begins to appear when the need for explanation or solution is intense; or when it kindles the curiosity of the researcher due to the shrouded mystery or controversy of the subject. To those who are already engaged in the field of research, selecting a research problem won't be a difficult task. Through the continuity of his deep, devoted work a researcher may come across many problems. Hence, for an experienced researcher, selecting a research problem may not pose problems so much as to a new comer. Further a research study concluded leads to further research by extending the possible areas of research. The task is always onerous to a new comer. He is always anxious to snatch a problem. In that process he may loose his balance and in a hurry he may land himself in difficulties. A research problem selected in haste more often leads to waste at later stages. *John Best,* an Educational Researcher cautions that, "the beginner is likely to select a problem that is much too broad in scope. This may be due to his lack of understanding of the nature of research and systematic problem-solving activity. It may also be due to his enthusiastic, but naive desire to solve an important problem quickly and immediately. Those who are more experienced know that research is often tedious, painfully slow and rarely spectacular. They realize that the search for truth and the solution of important problems take a great deal of time and energy and to intensive application of logical thinking:

The steps involved in the process of selection of research problems are:

Selection of a Problem for Research

This involves identification of a few problems and selecting one out of them, after evaluating the alternatives against certain selection criteria.

Formulation of the Selected Problem

The selected problem is defined and transformed into researchable questions.

Formulation of Hypotheses

The propositions to be tested are set up.

Conceptualization

The concepts associated with the problem under study are operationally defined and measurement devices are designed.

A research problem rightly and rationally selected solves half of the problem of research. The right selection of a topic has ultimate advantages and boosts the morale of the researcher. A right selection of a research problem helps the researcher to proceed in his work methodically and step by step. This paves the way to complete the project within the prescribed time limit and the cost can be rounded within the budgeted amount. A right selection also gives an enlightened picture of the problem at every stage, thereby avoiding as far as possible, unnecessary modification, omissions and additions. The seriousness of research will be kept alive throughout the period which ensures clarity of thinking, grasping of the concepts, logical analysis of data and justification of the title and objectives. In social science research when the project is at full steam, problems are bound to arise. Such problems could be reduced if the right topic, over which the researcher has mastery, is selected. Confusion at the selection level leads to confusion at every later stage, which ultimately results in the failure of the project.

Precautions to be taken while selecting a Research Problem

1. Select a topic in the field in which you have familiarity or in-depth understanding. "If the scholar is familiar with his field and knows what research has already been completed in it, he will also know something of the many problems that remain."
2. A research problem should be time bound and cost bound. Allowing scope for modifications in time and budget the scholars must complete the study within the limited period and cost. The selection of the topic must be made accordingly. A beginner can afford to choose only a simple problem. "The first topic will necessarily be a modest one, which can be carried on by an inexperienced researcher in a limited period of time. The emphasis will be placed upon the learning process, rather than on its actual contribution. This statement does not imply that the product is necessarily unimportant. It merely recognizes that the limitations of the first research project place the emphasis on learning how, with the hope that subsequent investigations will progressively yield more significant contributions to the advancement of knowledge."
3. The capacity of the research problem should be within the physical resources available to a researcher. Hence, a budget always forms part of a "Research Design" or "Research Proposal".

4. The basis for selection of the topic itself should be as strong as the foundation of a building which requires enormous reading, reference and discussion.
5. A researcher need not be in a hurry in choosing a problem. Carefully considered and objectively selected problems will imbibe confidence in a researcher. Spending considerable time to select a topic won't be a waste at all. It could very well save enormous time at later stages, which otherwise could not be available to a topic chosen in haste. *Best* advises that "Problem awareness is not ordinarily a characteristic of a beginner, and even the more experienced researcher approaches this step with hesitancy. It is a serious responsibility to commit oneself to a problem that will inevitably require much time and energy, and upon which so much academic significance is based.
6. While selecting a topic the researcher need not be over-enthusiastic. He must be balanced and must be ready to face unexpected twist, unreasonable delay, incompletion of data and subsequent second visit to the field. He should not feel the selected problem either too soft or two hard to deal with.

Pauline Young suggests that following points to be kept in mind while choosing a research topic:

1. Ability to grasp and time to deal with its broad implication.
2. Resources to carry the study forward may be exceedingly limited if no basic research has been previously done by experienced scientists in the field. At time resources are available, but they are not open to research beginners or they are confidential.
3. Applicability of study techniques should be considered for the particular topic chosen.
4. We should also consider degree of accuracy or approximation essential for the demands of scientifically conducted project.

What is a Research Problem?

As has been pointed out already, in social research, selection of problem must be given careful consideration and thorough scrutiny. The problem should have a purpose and worth appreciated in research terms. The problem must have intensity, must provided scope for deep analysis and must take smooth and orderly course of action. In other words, it must be a running stream and not a stagnant pool.

A problem can be called a research problem only when it satisfies the following conditions.

1. It must be worth studying. In other words, it must have viability or potentiality to stand as a research problem.
2. It must have social relevance. The study must be able to bring the attention of the experts, policy-makers; academicians etc, who are familiar with the subject.
3. There must be a 'felt need' for research over the problem. Such problem must be in need of further elaboration and exploration. As far as possible, it should be untouched by other researchers or even if touched must be in need of further research possibility.
4. A research problem must come out with pragmatic solutions to the issues.
5. As far as possible a social research problem must be up to date or relevant to the current social happenings; it should not be sterile.

Hillaway advocates the following rules to define a problem.

1. Be sure that the topic chosen is neither too vague nor too broad in scope.
2. To make the problem clearer and more understandable, state it as a question, this requires definite answer.
3. Carefully state that limitations of the problem,

eliminating all aspects and factors which will not be considered in the study.

4. Define any special terms that must be used in the statement of your problem.

How to Find a Research Problem?

For a researcher who is already engaged in research, selection of a topic will be an easier task. As he is able to come across variety of problems during the course of his studies in his field of specialization, he is in a position to choose a topic of his own choice and taste. But in the case of a beginner, to select a problem itself is problematical and he has to spend acquaint with relevant channels of research. In the course of his academic pursuit a researcher may come across many research problems. But many researchers, especially newcomers are in search of a problem. For such people, "Curiosity" for a problem of research study or "Curiosity about the unknown" is the best guide in selecting a problem. The enthusiasm that emanates at the beginning should sustain till the end of the research study. *Hillaway* is right when he says that, "a natural curiosity is the best guide in selecting a problem. The scholar usually decides to investigate a problem because it interests him, because he wants to know the solution. Further more he is likely to do a better job of research with a topic he selects because of the interest it holds for him than with one that is arbitrarily imposed.

Satisfaction of personal curiosity would seem, then, to be the most desirable incentive in the selection of a topic for study. This comes ordinarily, from having a thorough knowledge of one's field and of the gaps that exist in it."

A caution that is always given to a newcomer is not to select the problem in a hurry. It would be better if he spares more time in the selection than indulging in wasting time later on due to wrongful selection. If he spends some more time analyzing the viability of the topic, clarifying the thinking, achieving a sense of focus and reaching a stage from vagueness, to elucidation, he could precede his research orderly putting an end to unnecessary waste of time and resources. Careful selection of a topic and ultimate successful completion will sustain the researcher's keenness to research throughout his career.

Sources of Problems

The sources from which one may be able to identify research problems or develop problem awareness are:

Reading

When we critically study books and articles relating to subject of our interest, pertinent questions may arise in our mind. Similarly, areas of research may strike to our mind when we read research reports.

Academic Experience

Classroom lectures, class discussions, seminar discussions and out-of-class exchanges of ideas with fellow students and professors will suggest many stimulating problems to be studied.

Daily Experience

Life is dynamic. We learn new things and undergo new experiences every day. If we are alert, inquisitive and sensitive to life situation, we may hit upon/questions worth of investigation. "It is a mark of scientific genius to be sensitive to difficulties where less gifted people pass untroubled by doubt."

The story about Newton testifies to this. Apples have fallen on the heads of people before Newton's time, but it was the sensitive Newton who alone raised the question regarding fall of apple which led to his discovery of the law of gravitation.

Exposure to Field Situations

Field visits, internship training and extension work provide exposure to practical problems which call for study.

Consultations

Discussions with experts, teachers, administrators and business executives will help a researcher to identify meaningful problems for research.

Brain storming

Intensified discussion within a group of interested persons may often be a means of identifying pertinent questions, and of developing new ideas about a problem.

Research

Research on one problem may suggest problems for further research.

Intuition

Sometimes new ideas may strike to one's mind like a flash. Reflective mind is a spring of knowledge.

Process of identification

The process of identification of problem for academic research may consist of the following steps:

Selection of the Discipline

The subject in which one proposes to do research may be selected, e.g., Economics, Commerce, Management, Technology, Psychology etc. The selection of the discipline is easy. One can select any subject which one has studied thoroughly and which has interested him most. Where one has to do research in his field of specialization (e.g., Marketing) one has to choose the subject of one's specialization.

Demarcating the Broad Area or a Particular Aspect of the Selected Subject

The second step is to select a particular aspect of the selected subject. For example, if the selected subject is financial management, then one may select capital budgeting, financial leverage, working capital management or profit management as specific area of study.

One who says that he is willing to do research on any aspect of a discipline does not mean business or does not know oneself. One should identify one's specific interest. Interest in a particular area of a subject develops out of educational background, reading a good book or inspiration received from a professor.

Identifying Two or More Specific Topics in the Selected Broad Area

This is the final step in identification of problems. This requires a grasp of the branch of the subject as a whole and awareness of work already done on it. A review of concerned literature including research theses and survey of research published by the research councils like Indian Council of Social Science Research, New Delhi, intensive reading, reflective thinking, and discussion with the guide will help a student in identifying specific topics or issues for research. Both an uncharted path and a well-trodden path are dangerous to a beginner in research. If he chooses an unexplored problem, he has to grope in the dark and may get frustrated. On the other hand, if he selects problem which has already been thoroughly studied, he may not learn anything new nor contribute anything to the knowledge. It is desirable for him to adopt a via media approach. He may identify problems on which he can get the guidance of a few articles or books.

A student cannot just select anyone of the identified problems for his research. He has to evaluate them for choosing the most appropriate one. How can this evaluation be done? Against what criteria?

Criteria of Selection

The selection of one appropriate researchable problem out of the identified problems requires evaluation of those alternatives against certain criteria. These criteria may be grouped into:

(a) Internal (or personal) criteria or factors, and

(b) External criteria or factors.

Internal criteria consist of: *(i)* researcher's interest, *(ii)* researcher's competence, and *(iii)* researcher's own resource: finance and time.

External factors include *(i)* researchability of the problem, *(ii)* its importance and urgency, *(iii)* novelty of the problem, *(iv)* feasibility, *(v)* facilities, *(vi)* usefulness and social relevance, and *(vii)* research personnel.

Researcher's Interest

The problem should interest the researcher and be a challenge to him. Without interest and curiosity, he may not develop sustained perseverance. Even a small difficulty may become an excuse for discontinuing the study.

Interest in a problem depends upon the researcher's educational background, experience, outlook and sensitivity.

Researcher's Competence

A mere interest in a problem will not do. The researcher must be competent to plan and carry out a study of the problem. He must have the ability to grasp and deal with it. He must possess adequate knowledge of the subject – matter, relevant methodology and statistical procedures.

Researcher's Own Resources

In the case of a research to be done by a researcher on his own, consideration of his own financial resource is pertinent. Does the cost involved in conducting the study of the problem is within the means of the researcher? If it is beyond his means, he will not be able to complete the work, unless he gets some external financial support. Time resource is more important than finance.

Research is a time-consuming process. What is the time that the researcher can be able to spare for the research work? Is it adequate to meet the time requirements of the problem? If not, the work cannot be completed within the prescribed time constraints; it is desirable to over-estimate the time requirements and to under-estimate the time availability. In this connection, available tidbits of time (Say 5 or 10 minutes at a time) should not be conducted, as nothing could be done in 5 or 10 minutes, only large chunks of time available should be counted.

Researchability

The problem should be researchable, i.e., amenable for finding answers to the questions involved in it through scientific method. "Although every problem in science involves a question or a series of questions, not every question qualifies as a scientific problem." To be researchable a question must be one for which by observation or other data collection on the real world can provide the answer. Many questions cannot be answered on the basis of information alone. They may involve valve elements. E.g., what is merit for the purpose of employee promotion? What is 'fairness' to the workers? Some questions may not be reasonable because procedures or techniques are inadequate.

Importance and Urgency

Problems requiring investigation are unlimited, but available research efforts are very much limited. Therefore in selecting problems for research, their relative importance and significance should be considered. An important and urgent problem should be given priority over an unimportant one. For example, in industrial management today, problems of productivity, capacity utilization, motivation and industrial unrest are more important than problems of financial leverage, profit planning, vertical/horizontal integration, marketing etc. Research must be focused on useful and urgent problems.

Novelty or Originality

The problem must have novelty. There is no use of wasting one's time and energy on a problem already studied thoroughly by others.

This does not mean that replication is always needless. In social sciences in some cases, it is appropriate to replicate (repeat) a study in order to verify the validity of its findings to a different situation.

Feasibility

A problem may be a new one and also important, but if research on it is not feasible, it cannot be selected. Hence, feasibility is a very important consideration.

Facilities

Research requires certain facilities such as well-equipped library facility, suitable and competent guidance, data analysis facility, etc. Hence, the availability of the facilities relevant to the problem must be considered.

Usefulness and Social Relevance

Above all, the study of the problem should make significant contribution to the concerned body of knowledge or to the solution of some significant practical problem. It should be socially relevant. This consideration is particularly important in the case of higher level academic research and sponsored research.

Research Personnel

Research undertaken by professors and by research organizations require the services of investigators and research officers. But in India and other developing countries, research has not yet become a prospective profession. Hence, talented persons are not attracted to research projects. Employment in research projects is just considered as a stop gap arrangement pending securing a regular placement.

Therefore appropriate qualified and experienced research personnel are not easily available for the study of some problems.

The following resources are imperative in finding a research problem:

1. Physical resources
2. Monetary resources
3. Library resources

Physical Resources

Physical resources include the personal comforts, travel facilities etc. The problem area may be far away from the place of residence of the researcher and he has to spend considerable time and energy for that. So a comfortable travel arrangement is necessary. Clerical assistant, office help, communication facilities and stationary resources play no small role. Time is the foremost factor in choosing problem. A research study can be conducted within three moths and the same problem with broad nature and coverage can be undertaken for three years as well. As the social research is time bound, a topic must be selected in such a way to finish the study within the prescribed period. Universal experience is that social research always lags behind schedule. It is rare to come across studies completed within the prescribed time and budget. Both used to exceed their limits.

Monetary Resources

Next to time, monetary resources decide the selection of a research problem. A researcher can individually prepare the schedules, collect the data, and then write the report. When studies cover wider area, investigators must be appointed for data collection. Project experts must be employed and formation of an expert committee to guide the project may also be needed. Such projects are costlier and time consuming. But they carry with them accuracy, reliability and other concerned merits. So, depending upon the monetary resources available, a problem can be selected to cover limited or broader area. Its scope can also be limited or extended.

Library Resources

The prerequisite for a social research is library books, journals, periodicals, research reports, research journals, professional journals, bibliographies and indexes constitute flesh and blood for social research. "Not only will the scholar himself notice a number of unsolved, problem and unexplored areas during the course of his general study in his field, but he can frequently lay his hands on summaries and reviews of research that point these gaps out. Periodicals published for the scholar reader often contain long lists of topics upon which additional research is needed. Also from published articles and reports of research one can gain ideas and suggestions for subjects requiring further study. These aids can sometimes be of real help to the young scholar when he is looking about for a suitable problem to pick up. The annual bibliographies which appear in most fields of study will help to keep the scholar informed about the research continuing in his field. They may also suggest to him possible new areas for his own researches. Thus, even though the scholar probably cannot read every article listed in the annual bibliography, he can at least gather a fairly accurate picture or what his contemporaries in the field have been doing and this in turn should give him ideas for subjects to study for himself."

One of the useful sources of selecting a research problem is to visit National Institutes and Research Institutes engaged in the field of research in particular field. Going through the library and contracting the scholars and such institutes will definitely give confidence to the researcher in selecting a problem.

10

Research Gap in Social Science Research

Research Gap is in important area of research which a researcher should not forget to recognize its merits. Hell of confusions could be avoided if this concept is understood in proper perspective by researchers. 'Research gap' in social sciences is referred to the 'unexplored area of research or areas of research which has not been touched by others so far. In other words research gap points out the following significances in a research area/programme:

1. It induces the involvement of the researcher in the task of mastering the areas/topics where research has been already undertaken.
2. Scope for creativity is created on the part of the researcher to refer all sources of publication and exhaust the review of literature.

Present Condition

The present condition of selecting a research problem by researchers in the field of social sciences is very pathetic and riddled with repetition. Young researchers as well as experienced teachers, with few exceptions, want the process of selecting a research problem to be completed without any labour and majority of them leave this important task of research to their supervisors. Many research guides/ supervisors on their part simply impose or dictate topics of research to their wards without knowing the potentiality and hard work of their wards or they don't want to put their wards under the ordeal of 'selecting a problem' process. Given the option and a freehand, many scholars take lot of time to locate a suitable research problem or end in confusion or go for the simple mechanism of selecting a problem already done. Such process never encourages the fundamental basics of research, 'curiosity about the unknown'. Efforts must be put forward to know more about the unknown and the voyage to find out new facts or truth must be as that of the sailor lyses.

Importance of Research Gap

Research gap tells a researcher 'what to do' and 'what not to do'. It needs tremendous labour and meticulous observation of past work done by various researchers. More library reference will not do justification. Using of reference/ bibliography cards and sources cards would be of immense help to them. This must be preceded by listing of books and journals in the field. If a particular book or journal is not available all other important libraries must be searched. Spending time and effort on such endeavour is not a waste compared to resting on others' efforts of copying another bibliography.

Consultation with experts in the field is another way of locating a 'research gap'. A honest and right thinking expert will definitely guide you in the areas to be searched. Referring foreign journals and foreign experts are additional sources, but they are time consuming and laborious job. A researcher has to come out of his 'shell' and have a open and frank mind of locating 'new vistas of knowledge' rather than beating round the bush.

Locating the research gap has multifaceted advantages to the researcher. One basic advantage is it avoids the wastage of resources. Availability of time is a crucial factor for a scholar and saving time is equal to that of saving money. Past experience in the field of social research has shown that rarely scholars complete their work in time. One of the stumbling blocks for a scholar is spending enormous time in selecting the topic of research. Providing clarity, narrow downing the scope, conceptual clarifications, etc. have to be evenly justified by a scholar in the selection process. For such purpose a side support is provided by the research gap. Hence, time as a vital resource is served by the location of research gap.

Research gap avoids repetition of research problems, methodologies and even findings. Today's bane of social research is repetition of research area and the fallout is stereo typed research findings. These things must be avoided and innovative findings must come out. These are the days of 'action research' which warrants the need to do research which are socially relevant. Any amount of money and time spent on research must have practical utility to society. This practical utility of resources of social research can be gained out of locating research gap and finding new and fresh areas of research.

While locating the research gap a researcher gains a lot by means of expanding his creativity and thinking faculty. Creative thinking and probing nature will provide greater scope for locating new areas of research.

11

Study of Related Literature

Study of related literature is an important part at the stage of selecting a research problem as well as at later stages of research process. While selecting a research problem the researcher has to familiarize with his area of field of research. Wider knowledge about the field is essential to understand the very area of research. One should be a voracious reader and should create depth in the field of specialization. Shallow reading cannot help as the researcher is expected to be familiar with new concepts and theories. Study of related literature has two stages, the first one is used for general study. The second stage is reviewing the previous research studies in the same area or closely related areas of research.

Need to Study Literature

1. Going through relevant literature a researcher can gain theoretical knowledge.
2. Study of related literature helps to familiarize oneself with the existing knowledge, and various types of research studies undertaken in the field.
3. Innovations, latest developments, new tools of research can be identified by reviewing literature.

4. New concepts and variables can be located.
5. By reviewing relevant literature the 'Research gap' can be identified. Through this process the researcher can fill the gap and can avoid repetition.
6. To frame effective hypothesis review of literature is needed.
7. One can differentiate one's research problem from others. Thereby you can establish the unique nature of your study.
8. Relevant methodology and tools of data collection can be decided.
9. Appropriate statistical tools can also be determined by going through relevant literatures.

Definition of Literature

A researcher has to go through various types of literature like books, journals, committee reports, institutional reports, etc. Any type of literature that is used, referred or abstracted forms part of literature.

Stages of referring Literature

1. The first stage is at which the researcher has to gain familiarity with the 'Area of Research'. It is to know, what is what?
2. Second stage is to identify the research problem as such. This process is undertaken after establishing the 'research gap' in the field. As far as possible the research problem must be defined suitably and its scope must be pinpointed.
3. Next stage is the 'Operationalisation of concepts'. This process helps to identify suitable concepts and variables needed for the study.
4. Framing of hypothesis is the next stage where one has to refer previous research studies.
5. While preparing the 'Research design' or 'Research

proposal' one has to go through various literature.

6. For the construction of tools for data collection and for deciding the right type of statistical tools review of literature is essential.
7. While writing the theoretical chapter or portions of the report, reference of various materials is a must.
8. After writing the final report bibliography has to be collected, which is possible through the preparation of 'Source Cards.'

Precautions to be Followed

1. Make it a habit to go through literature from the beginning to the end of the research process.
2. Study the materials thoroughly.
3. Keep source cards ready and note things then and there.
4. Record only materials needed for your study.
5. Must be able to distinguish 'needed sources' and 'unwanted sources'.
6. Any source taken must be acknowledged. Abrupt copying amounts to plagiarism.
7. Keep all the cards safer even after your research work is over.
8. Continue the habit of referring sources even after your research work is over as you are expected to become an authority in your area of research by means of publishing more research papers, undertaking independent research works, guiding scholars or writing books.

12

Interaction with Literature—Research Journals

A literature may be taken to include all that is recorded and available in the manuscript or printed from—official and non-official. Such literatures may provide detailed information which may be basic, advanced and operational and which are available in libraries, offices and archives etc. Consulting literature in research either extensively or intensively is called interaction with literature. Such interaction begins for identifying research problems and destines at the research reporting. Literatures are secondary sources which form the first working base for outlining the problems and analysis. A recognized literature is a beacon for research in alleviating problems.

The Forms of Interaction

Interaction with literature can be generally made through different channels. In the process of research, knowledge on the sources of information, collection and establishing contact are the various dimensions. The sources are:

(i) Subject Catalogue

The catalogue maintained in libraries—subject-wise open up new vistas. The researcher can have exhaustive collection of item of various books/journals concentrating on the main and sub-themes. This will facilitate access to vital documents too. In the case of inter-disciplinary research, consultation of related subject will contribute for the accomplishment of the desired objective.

(ii) Documentation Support Service

Catering to the special requirements of research, documentation support services are available. Under one roof, at a time, the scholars can have access to materials which appeared in literatures. This source provides a long list of the journals/magazines/reports/publications available on different subjects of choice on payment basis. These services are also offered by specialized centers for the benefit of research scholars in varied disciplines. Some of them specializing in social science are: *(a)* Social Science Documentation Centre, ICSSR, New Delhi, *(b)* National Documentation Centre, New Delhi, *(c)* Small Enterprises Documentation Centre, Hyderabad, *(d)* Centre for Rural Documentation, Hyderabad, *(e)* NCAER, New Delhi, *(f)* Centre for Economic and Social Study, Hyderabad.

(iii) Journals

Journals regional, national and international, are the carriers of latest sources of information on research providing insider information to different places at a time. Conceptual changes, findings, innovations are disseminated largely through this source. Hence, interactions with journals are a sine-qua-non. Hence, journals form a core source of information.

(iv) Government Reports

Consultation with report of the Government, Enquiry Committee, Study Teams, Special Task Force on policy implications and execution form part of other elements in spectrum. The Controller of Publications (Government of India) brings out a number of publications. Some of them are Administration Reports, Statistical Reports, Bills, Acts, Law Reports etc. Publication by other agencies such as Reserve Bank of India, Reports of Financial Institutions, Ministries of the Government of India such as Finance, Industries, Foreign Trade, Handicrafts and Handlooms, Social Welfare to cite a few are other relevant sources.

(v) Research Abstracts

Access to research abstracts helps to know the work. An abstract provides pertinent, bibliographical details such as title, author, periodicity, publisher etc., besides providing a brief outline of the research, methodology adopted, and findings of research. ICSSR Research Quarterly, Indian Dissertation Abstracts on ICSSR, ICSSR Journal of Abstracts and Reviews of Sociology, Abstract and Review in Economics, Geography, and Political Science etc. are some of them. Data India, Committees and Commissions in India (1947-73) – a 10 volume digest edited by Virendra Kumar, Statistical Abstract – India, Public Undertakings Digest of News and Views are yet other abstracts providing information.

(vi) Information Source on Research Already Done

Interaction on the dissertation already available will throw new lights to researchers in eliminating the area already covered by others, identification of newer ones. Scope for further research in terms of quantitative and qualitative analysis can well be planned through this kind of interaction. Some of the sources which can be tapped for ascertaining the information are: *(a)* Bibliography of Doctoral Dissertations accepted by Indian Universities on Social Sciences, *(b)* Theses on Indian Subcontinents (1879 to 1971), *(c)* Foreign Theses on India, Mimeographed Publication of ICSSR, *(d)* University News, Fortnightly Publication of Association of Indian Universities indicating the Doctoral theses accepted by various Indian universities, Ph.D. theses in progress.

Interaction With Journals—Outcome

Journals are periodicals carrying matters relating to current events in the field of specialization. The journals provide narrative material, statistical data, methods of analysis and interpretations in capsule forms

Interactions with journals by researchers keep abreast of knowledge in the field. Further, annual numbers and back volumes become an invaluable asset for any time reference paying way for updating the knowledge. Hence, it enables relating the contemplated investigation of earlier efforts, thus preventing repetition of research projects. It would also facilitate hypothesis formulation and suggest new avenues of approach, induction to unknown field etc.

A research journal can provide quotable quotes of authors and eminent personalities which are widely used for citation/ evidencing/endorsing similar views in varied contexts, situations and ground realities. The basic data published in journals relating to the specific areas of research, can be of immense use. Such data can be used for inter and intra-comparison purpose particularly under ANOVA. Hence, it is preferable to go for subscription of prominent and core journals which will provide data/ information at the door steps of the scholars, leading to saving in effort, time and money largely.

Latest theories, application can well be accessed in journals. It is acclaimed as one of the fastest and quick source of transmission of information/data to the desired sector of research. Similarly, empirical verification for collaborating the theories, the confrontations can be spelt out through this media

In some disciplines, research through publications and their universal acceptance of the findings are considered vital for the award of research degrees particularly in the field of physical and biological sciences. Hence, the journals are accepted as windows of research.

Interaction with Journals through Internet

In the dynamic world there is an increasing opportunity to consult the journals far and near through internet links. A scholar in one place can have easy access for information available in any library/archive anywhere in the world and can get copies in no time. This resulted in saving time and avoiding communication distortion.

The University Grants Commission (UGC) has initiated a programme to provide electronic access to over the internet to scholarly literature in all areas of learning to the university sector in India. The programme is wholly funded by the UGC. All universities which come under UGC's purview will be members of the programme, and it will gradually be extended to colleges as well. The programme is being executed by Director, Information and Library Network (INFLIBNET) Centre, Ahmedabad which is an autonomous institution under the UGC. Access to various E-Journals has started from January 1, 2004. The E-Journals programme aims at covering all fields of learning of relevance including

- Arts, Humanities and Social Sciences
- Physical and Chemical Sciences
- Life Sciences
- Computer Science, Mathematics, Statistics

Access is provided to current as well as archival literature. Portals are provided which will enable users to navigate easily through all the literature that is made available.

When to Consult a Research Journal?

The most abridge and capsule form of answer to this question is consultation at anytime. For selecting the area, identification of topic precisely, survey of literature, hypothesis formulation, preparing the interview schedule/ mailed questionnaire, theory building, tabulation of data, interpretation and up to the stage of writing the thesis consultation is inevitable and imperative.

Indexing the Content

Access to the journal will not serve any purpose unless the research scholar acquires the information/data and uses them at the appropriate time and place. Efforts can be made to keep the data for any time use through some kind of arrangement. An easy way to bring the content in the thesis is through preparation of card index of items interacted. Classification of information/data according to the objectives of the study and chapter arrangements, will unfailingly yield good result.

13

Interaction with the Experts

Research is a very much pleasant and beautiful experience. It ought to be because; the person who is doing the research is going to be a contributor to the society in which he is existing. Realizing this fact a research scholar should be careful enough to adopt right methods and approaches in all disciplines of a research task.

One of the disciplines of the research is the work of collection of data. It is nothing but the collection of facts for evolving the theory. Of course, this work has it momentum throughout the research period after the major work of selecting the topic. Sometimes, we may have to get some important data even after completing the research.

The work of collection of data includes many disciplines like consulting both primary and secondary sources, issuing questionnaires and conducting interviews. But for shaping the knowledge, he has to depend upon the experts.

Interacting with the experts of the field in which the scholar is undertaking the research gives new lights to scholars. This work needs a kind of both mental and physical preparations. Of course, the interaction can be conducted with the people who are all considered to be resourceful and helpful in general.

Even though, for each and every interaction, he should go with sufficient preparation, he should be most careful in facing the experts.

The scholar should prepare himself both mentally and physically for this endeavour. First it is important for the scholar to prepare himself mentally.

He has to keep few things in his mind.

1. This is an incomparably significant discipline, in spite of having chances for errors and bias in the information. The sharing of the experiences of the experts in person, receiving the pieces of advice and the expert guidelines will help to proceed with the research in proper perspective.
2. The scholar must understand that a conversation is going to take place in the interactions which is going to benefit him only. So he must give place for emotional split at any moment.
3. It is also important to keep in mind that the interview is to elicit the required information from the experts only and not to educate him. Hence, to make the work as the most successful one, the scholar must adopt certain formal interaction process which are inevitable.

The Formal Interaction Process

Accessibility

The expert, who is interacted, is supposed to be enriched with the information about the field of the scholar and to provide the required information to the scholar.

But this may be affected on account of several reasons like below:

(i) The expert has forgotten the required information on account of his physical problems like old age and weak memory and non-familiar with the specific area of the scholar at the moment.

(ii) The expert would have got some emotional stress which may prevent him from revealing the information. During such kind of situations, the scholar should be careful in dealing with the experts. He has to study the mind of the experts very much carefully.

(iii) There is much possibility for rising up of certain situations that the experts are not willing to share their views, on account of having different ideas about the subject. At the time, the scholar should be very much careful in undertaking the interaction programmes with experts.

Cognition

This process occupies the second place of the formal interview procedures. Cognition is nothing but the understanding of the role of the expert on the occasion of interview. This should be given by the scholar to the expert already in a proper manner. Before the interview the scholar should ensure it.

Motivation

This process is the most important process which makes the whole attempt a successful one.

This scholar should give perfect motivation to the expert about the interview on three backgrounds.

1. *Motivation for initial decision to cooperate:* This motivation provides the idea in the mind of the expert to cooperate with scholar for making the attempt a successful one.
2. *Subsequent decision to continue:* While the interaction is carried on, the motivation should be given to the expert subsequently that he should give more information to the scholar in order to help him. He should give accurate and sufficient information avoiding the distorted replies.

The scholar must have patience to prepare himself for

the task by having enough training for him. If he is able to prepare himself mentally, it is much possible for him to prepare himself physically.

Some of the ideas for the scholars for preparing himself physically:

1. Dressing up in impressive manner
2. Go with suitable equipments for the interviews
3. Avoid mannerisms
4. Tone or voice should be soft
5. Avoid distractions.

14

Methods of Sampling

In all research studies, to select the respondents, sampling is used. As the population or the universe involved will be large, it is impossible to contact all of them. As human beings have certain homogeneous nature among themselves, it is enough if we meet few of them as they will have the representative nature for the population. Sampling as a technique has been widely used by marketing researchers, as they have to cover a population spread in wider geographical area.

The social scientist is confronted with the task of investigating vast population. Sampling is a method to make social investigation practicable and easy. According to Goode and Hatt: 'A sample is a smaller representation of the larger whole.'

Blalock and Blalock define a sample thus: "It is a small piece of the population obtained by a probability process that mirrors, with known precision, the various patterns and sub-classes of the population."

Ya-Lun-Chou defines a sample, "as a collection of primary sampling units selected as a representative microcosm from which references about the population may be made."

The above definitions contain three important implications as listed out by Ya-Lun-Chou:

Firstly a sample may contain primary sampling units such as firms of an industry, even though its purpose is to observe the properties of the elementary units such as the workers in the industry. Secondly, a sample is not chunk or a slice of the population selected because of convenience and ready availability, but a microcosm, a small universe or a subject which is expected to be representative of the parent population. Third and last, the ultimate purpose of sampling is not merely to secure sample statistics but to make inferences concerning the population.

Advantages of Sampling

Sampling has certain obvious advantages. They are:

1. Sampling avoids the necessity of studying each and very member of the population and thus avoids necessary wastage of time and resources by collecting large quantities of data from large number of people.
2. It ensures greater precision and contributes to the quality of data as it facilitates the collection of smaller amounts of data from fewer cases and their intensive analysis.
3. Sampling if properly drawn to represent a cross-section of the population, will give an accurate estimation of the population. It is said that, appropriate sampling, gives greater accuracy than even the complete enumeration by census.

Requirements of a Good Sample

The main requirements of a good sample are:

1. Representativeness
2. Adequacy
3. Avoiding Bias

1. *Representativeness*

Representativeness denotes the reflection of certain characteristics of the sample as that of the universe or population. When selecting a sample the researcher must have complete details of the population. Haphazard method will lead to waste of time and resources.

2. *Adequacy*

According to *Goode and Hatt,* "a sample is adequate when it is of sufficient size to allow confidence in the stability of its characteristics." In other words it should not be too large than is necessary.

3. *Avoiding Bias*

According to *Moser and Kalton* bias in selection of sample can arise:

(i) If the sample is done by a non-random method which generally means that the selection is consciously or unconsciously influenced by human choice;

(ii) If the sampling frame (list, index or other population record) which serves as the basis for selection does not cover the population adequately, completely or accurately.

(iii) If some sections of the population are impossible to find or refuse to cooperate."

The best method to avoid bias in sampling is to use random method of sampling. Delens gives the following features of good sample:

(1) A sample should not only be designed to produce the actual information required by the study but must also provide an adequate basis for the measurement of its own reliability.

(2) A sample should be large enough to provide sub-samples of size adequate for the proper analysis of subsidiary problems.

Type of Samples

The various methods of sampling may broadly be classified into two categories namely: *(a)* Probability Sampling and *(b)* Non-Probability Sampling.

Probability Sampling

The probability sampling implies that each unit of the population has the same chance or probability of selection. Simple Random sampling, Systematic Sampling and cluster sampling are considered as probability sampling.

Non-Probability Sampling

The non-probability sampling which is also called Judgment sampling, is based on the personal judgment. Elements included in a judgment sample are results of the investigator's expert judgment as to their representativeness. Consequently the probability of each individual element being included in the sample is not known. Sampling method can be broadly categorized as below:

1. Simple Random Sampling

According to Parten: "Random sampling is the term applied when the method of selection assures each individual element in the universe an equal chance of being selected."

Thus, the unit in the population under simple random sampling is provided an equal chance of being selected. As *Moser* aptly puts it: "Equity not be misunderstood as a haphazard, unprincipled selection. It is a methodical selection.

Features of Simple Random Sampling

1. Items in the sample are selected completely independent of each other, which means that the selection of one unit does not influence the selection of others, positively or negatively.
2. It is a probability sample. Each item has the same chance of being selected. As stated by *Goode & Hatt:*

"The units of the universe are so arranged that the selection process gives equi-probability of selection to every unit in that universe."

3. It is purely a chance of selection but it is not haphazard or hit and miss selection. Deliberate methods are used to ensure chance of selection.
4. There is absolutely no room for bias of any kind in the selection of sample units. There cannot be any conscious selection.

Principles of Simple Random Sampling

Parten in her famous book "Surveys, Polls and Samples" lays down some important principles to be followed in adopting simple random sampling. They are:

1. Population and the units must be clearly defined.
2. The units must consist of large number of small units.
3. The universe must consist of large number of small units.
4. Units must be independent of each other.
5. List of the universe must be got ready.
6. Methods of selection should be completely independent of the characteristics to be examined.
7. Units drawn should be accessible for investigation.
8. Once selected the unit cannot be discarded.

Procedure of Selection

While selecting the sample units following are the procedures to be adopted.

First of all serial numbers are allotted to each member of the universe. Secondly, selecting the serial number of units on either of the following modes:

1. Random number tables, which will be available in any book on statistics.

2. Drawing by lot numbered slips of paper from container, either with or without replacement. It is always preferable to make selection with replacement to ensure probability and independence of selection.

Thirdly using the units of the population whose serial numbers are selected for the purpose of study.

Advantages

This method has several advantages. They are:

1. No advance knowledge of the characteristics of the population is necessary.
2. Assessment of the accuracy of the results is possible by sample error estimation.
3. It is representative of the universe.
4. Bias due to human preferences and influences is estimated.
5. It is a simple and easily practicable procedure if the population is not large.
6. It is less expensive.

Limitations

Simple random sampling has got certain practical difficulties and inherent limitations, which are as follows:

1. Definition of the universe in many times is inadequate.
2. The ready lists of universe are not always available; serializing the large population is also difficult.
3. Sampling is likely to be biased at the survey stage due to non-response or non-availability of the sample units.

2. *Stratified Random Sampling*

It is a sampling plan which attempts to design a more efficient sample. It retains the random element, at the same time; it is more representative of the population. It is a method used for increasing the precision of sampling. According to this method, first the population is divided into homogeneous groups or strata and sample is drawn from each stratum. Ya-Lum-Chun defines stratified random sampling thus: "The Process of stratification requires that the population is divided into groups or classes called strata. Then a sample is taken from each stratum by simple random method and the resulting samples is called a stratified sample." The basis of classification is anything such as sex, education, income, land holding etc., which is known as stratification factor. The stratification factor is selected in correlation with the problem under study, which becomes a logical basis of stratification. For instance, if adoption of improved agricultural practices is studied, then naturally size of sample is taken. Disproportionate sampling includes equal number of samples from each stratum. A proportional stratification yield a sample that represents the universe in the same proportion in which each stratum is represented in the population.

Principles of Stratification

The stratified random sample has to observe certain basic principles, particularly at the time of stratification. They are:

1. There must be as much uniformity as possible within each stratum i.e., homogeneity.
2. There should be as great differences as possible among various stratum i.e. heterogeneity or variability.

Advantages

1. Stratified sampling is more representation of the population.
2. It is more precise and to a great extent avoids bias.
3. It saves time and cost of data collection since the sample size can be less in this method.
4. It is geographically concentrated and renders data collection convenient.

Disadvantages

1. It requires the knowledge of the traits of the population.
2. Classification or stratification becomes sometimes difficult and still difficult in the assignment of each unit of the population to a particular stratum.
3. The results sometimes have to be weighted according to the size of strata, which is a difficult task.
4. Preparing a stratified list is an arduous task as the lists may not be readily available.

3. *Systematic Sampling*

Systematic sampling is a frequently used sampling plan. According to this method, sample is taken from a list prepared on a systematic arrangement either on the basis of alphabetic order, or on house number or any other method. Strictly speaking it is not a random sampling, though it includes an element of random selection. Therefore it is sometimes called quasi-random sampling. If simple random sampling cannot be adopted for some reason, systematic sampling is an alternative method, since it is reasonably accepted as equivalent to random sampling.

Steps in Systematic Sampling

1. First of all the population is given serial number from I to N.
2. The sampling interval is determined by dividing the population by the size of the sample i.e., N=K.
3. Any number is selected at random from the first sampling intervals.
4. The subsequent samples are selected at equal and regular intervals.

For example, let the size of the population be, 1000: and the sample size be 100. These 100 samples are to be drawn from the population numbering 1000. The sample interval is 10. Suppose the first sample selected at random from the first interval is 6, then the subsequent samples are 16, 26, 36, 46, 56 and so on. Thus, in the systematic sampling the initial start is made on random basis which determines the subsequent samples. The randomness is retained at only one stage.

Advantages

1. It is a simple design and easy to execute.
2. Randomness and probability features are present which make the sample representative.

Disadvantages

1. As in simple random, the population has to be serialized in this sample also, which becomes a difficult task when the population is huge.
2. Any hidden periodicity in the list will adversely affect the representativeness of the sample.
3. There is always a temptation to reselect or restart while making selection.

4. Cluster Sampling

Cluster sampling refers to the procedure of dividing the population into groups called clusters and drawing a sample of clusters to represent the population. A cluster may consist of either the primary sample units or elementary secondary sample units. In a selected cluster either all the sample units are selected or a few of them are chosen on any sampling method. For instance, if a study has to be made on the industrial workers of a district, the industrial units are the primary sample units. If the primary sample units clustering in one particular locality is selected then it forms the first stage cluster; and when workers employed in one or two firms are selected that forms the second stage cluster. A plan to make selection of clusters within clusters is called multi-stage cluster sampling. Thus, one significant factor that differentiates the cluster sampling from other methods of sampling is that unlike in other types of samples in which each element in the population is separately selected, in the cluster sampling, groups are selected. A cluster may be anything, a school, municipal ward, an industry or a cooperative society.

Principles of Cluster Sampling

The participles that are basis to the cluster sampling method is just opposite to those governing the stratified sampling. These principles are essential to ensure maximum efficiency in sampling.

1. The differences or variability within a cluster should be as large as possible i.e., heterogeneity.
2. The variability among or between groups or clusters should be as small as possible i.e., homogeneity.

Advantages

1. This method provides significant cost gain.
2. It is easy and more practical method, which facilitates the field work.
3. Because of the geographical contiguity of the sample more units can be included.

Disadvantages

1. Probability and representiveness of the sample is sometimes affected.
2. The results are likely to be less precise and accurate.

5. Sampling with Varying Probabilities

It is also known as the sampling with probability proportionate to size. This is an important sampling plan applied in multi-stage selection. It ensures that the probability of selection of any sample is proportionate to the size of the group. That means, we have more chance of selecting samples from larger groups than from small groups. After assigning appropriate sample size, proportionate to the size of the cluster, a systematic selection is made at the second stage. For example, if the members of cooperative societies are our secondary sample units, the respective cooperative societies with varying size of membership are the primary sample units or first stage cluster. The probability of selection is given according to the size of membership by adopting the following steps:

1. Listing the cooperative societies selected.
2. Listing the membership strength of each society.
3. Entering their cumulative total.
4. Calculating the sampling interval.

Size of population i.e.,

Size of sample

5. Systematic Selection at Equal Intervals

The following example with clarify the point

Cooperative Society	*No. of Members*	*Cumulative Total*	*Selected Sample Units*
1	200	200	20, 80, 140, 200
2	100	300	260,
3	300	600	320, 380, 440, 500, 560
4	500	1100	620, 680, 740, 800, 860, 220, 980, 1040, 1100
5	400	1500	1160, 1220, 1280, 1340, 1400, 1460
6	700	2200	1520, 1580, 1640, 1700, 1760, 1820, 1880, 1940, 2020, 2080, 2140, 2200
7	50	2250	2260
8	150	2400	2320, 2380
9	350	2750	2420, 2480, 2540, 2600, 2660, 2720
10	250	3000	2780, 2840, 3000

The cumulative total is made as shown in the above table and the sample interval is decided as in the case of systematic sampling. In this case the sample size is fixed as 50 and sample interval becomes 60 (i.e.,) 3,000 = 60. The random start is given 20 and the subsequent samples are systematically selected at equal interval as shown in the above table.

Advantages

1. It is helpful in giving the group with large number of units, greater probability of selection and thereby making the sample more representative.
2. It is an appropriate sampling plan in finding out the variability of groups.

Limitations

1. Listing and totaling of sampling involves elaborate work.
2. This sample is more appropriate in two-stage or multi-stage sampling plan.

6. Area Sampling

Area sampling is very much similar to the multi-stage cluster sampling. One special feature of area sampling is that the basis of selection is the map rather than the list of population. The basic technique in area sampling is to divide the primary sampling units such as district, development block, revenue village, municipal ward etc. For example from a city map one or two wards are selected where from a compete enumeration of households is made or a sample of households are studied. Likewise from a district map one or two development blocks are chosen and from each block, one or two revenue village segments may be enumerated completely or a sample household may be studied.

Steps

1. Stratification of the primary sampling units on the basis of geographical area.
2. Selection of primary sampling units from each stratum.
3. Sub-sampling of small units within each stratum.
4. Enumeration of household.

Advantages

1. Survey work can be conducted with considerable speed.
2. It is reliable and satisfactory as complete enumeration is involved.

Disadvantages

1. It is fairly expensive.
2. It also involves considerable amount of listing of areas and sub-areas, though complete listing of households or individuals is not necessary.

7. Quota Sampling

Quota sampling is one of the commonly used methods of sampling in market surveys and opinion polls. Though basically it is a non-random sampling, this method combines the aspects of probability sampling and purposive selection. Following are the three basic steps in quota sampling:

1. First the population is stratified on some basis, preferably on the basis of the characteristics of the population pertaining to the study.
2. Determination of the proportion of the population falling in each stratum.
3. The quota of sample units is decided and assigned for each stratum.

Advantages

1. It is a practical as well as a convenient method.
2. It is economical.
3. It is the only useful method when no sample frame is available.

Disadvantages

1. It is unreliable and prone to bias.

2. It is not a representative sample.
3. It is not possible to estimate the standard error.
4. Control of field work is difficult.

8. Purposive Sampling

Due to certain practical difficulties, it may not be always possible to follow probability sampling. In that case the researcher will look for an alternative sampling plan which will ensure representative sampling. When he decides to select a sub-group which is a 'barometer' or representative of the whole population, it is called a purposive selection. Thus, the selection of the sample units is left to the choice or discretion of the researcher. But it is ensured that the selected units are the representative of the universe. As defined by *Jensen:* "purposive selection denotes the method of selecting a number or groups of units in such a way that the selected groups together yield as nearly as possible the same average or proportion as the totality with respect to the characteristics which are already a matter of statistical knowledge." In short the selected units must be typical.

Advantages

1. It is a practical method when randomization is not possible.
2. Enumeration is quick and economical.

Disadvantages

1. Considerable prior knowledge of the population is necessary.
2. Estimation of sampling error is not possible.

15

Developing Research Competencies through Attending Relevant Seminars/ Workshops

Seminar/workshop is the gateway through which the research experts bring to light their research findings. It would enable the participants to understand the methodology employed and the results arrived at by the researchers. It would also enable the researchers to highlight the practical difficulties encountered and their perseverance and dedication to the research.

A research finding is said to be good, if it is acclaimed, appreciated and accepted by majority of the participants who are specialized in the similar field of research.

The participants of any seminar/workshop can be grouped into: *(i)* the young researchers, *(ii)* the resource person and *(iii)* the sponsoring agency.

Finding solution to the existing as well as the emerging problem the society should be the chief objective for conducting any seminar/workshop.

No Agency to Coordinate the Seminar/Workshop

There has been no coordination among the sponsoring agencies while conducting seminars/workshop though we have many sponsoring agencies at the national as well as regional level.

In these days, the environment of the people is getting changed rapidly and it affects the social, cultural, political and economic life of the people.

Accordingly we have research problem relating to social, cultural, political and economic activities. The complexities and dimensions of these problems are not uniform and equal.

For instance, in the field of economics, the research experts conduct research on various subjects viz., economics of institutions, employment and savings, production and market, budget and taxes, export and import and plethora of other economic activities. No mechanism has so far been found by any agency to determine the order of importance of these activities and which of them need immediate solution from the subject experts.

At times the field experts do conduct research on those problems which need less attention and fail to concentrate on some of the vital issues which need immediate research findings.

From this perspective, there is a need for some agencies to coordinate the research activities and highlight the problems of the society which need immediate attention.

The deterioration of the quality of research is due to the absence of any agency which controls, regulates and monitors research work. A well coordinated body comprising academics, business houses and Government should be constituted by the Government. They should plan out the broad subjects on which micro studies may be taken up. Regional studies are the need of the hour for the planning purpose.

Otherwise the very purpose of research will be defeated; whatever may be the objective of the study. Research is being done for the research sake. In these days the number of theses is getting increased. However the results that come out of them are not commensurate with the number of theses. Inadequate knowledge in research methodology dilutes the quality of the research findings and the quality has come down to its lower ebb. How to employ appropriate research methodology is still a grey area which needs attention of the experts.

We are living in the age of computers. We avail the excellent services of computers for the data processing, tabulation and interpretation. Computers reduce the physical strain of the researchers. However they fail to concentrate on certain other activities viz., personal observation, in-depth review of literature, etc.

The success of any research depends upon the individual's aptitude in the research. There is no tool to measure the quantum of work to be done and the minimum and maximum work to be exerted for a given study. To what extent, the researchers have to spare time, the clarity they need, the depth of knowledge they gain, before they bring out research results need some sort of clarity.

Attending relevant seminar/workshop is the only remedy for the participants to find solution to the above listed problems. Keeping this in mind, an attempt has been made to discuss about the development of research competencies attending relevant seminars/workshops.

What is Seminar/Workshop?

Seminar means a small group of researchers engaged in advanced study and original research under a member of the faculty meeting regularly to exchange information and hold discussions.

Workshop means a seminar, discussion group or the like which emphasizes exchange of ideas and the demonstration and application of techniques, skills etc.

Conference—we mean the art of conferring or consulting together, consultation especially on an important or serious matter.

The Participants

The participants include the resource persons, the organizers, the sponsoring agency, the young researchers and the target audience. From the researchers' point of view the attendance of seminar/workshop depends upon the research experts. The experts are the pioneers in their respective field of study. The advancement of any subject purely depends upon the active involvement of experts. Young researchers must see who the subject experts are and who present the papers in the seminar/workshops.

The participants of seminars/workshops mostly consist of aspiring young researchers. They expect to find research topics in the seminar for probing further. In these days scholars as well as supervisors who do not attend seminars/ workshops at frequent intervals find difficulty of choosing the research topics. It is a ticklish issue. Those who attend seminars at regular intervals have a long list of topics which are amenable for research. In these days, the theses presented in the universities are stereo-typed and examiners are reluctant to value them and simply return the same by saying that 'preoccupied with other engagements'. Those who attend seminars never feel dearth of research topics. The gist of research papers presented in the seminar throws more light on the new areas of research.

Instead of familiarizing with the existing review of literature and find out the gap for further research, it would be an alternate for the scholars to select topics which are declared as 'gap' in the seminars/workshops.

Experts focus the subjects from two angles viz., *(i)* the existing problems and finding solutions to it, and *(ii)* the development of new techniques. The young scholars may attend those seminars/workshops where the experts focus their attention to the problems.

The subject experts highlight the grey areas which need the attention of the researchers at the micro level. For instance, there is a problem in the field of management due to globalization. Hitherto the subject describes the management of people/personnel of the respective nation.

Now we need managers to know as how to understand the intricacies and complications to be involved in the managing of people of different nations, different language and different culture who come to work together. The subject experts of the Harvard University now direct their attention towards the development of new strategy in this regard.

Thus, attending relevant seminars would enable the scholars to find not the experts but also a suitable guide/ supervisor for their further study.

Present research work is aimless, haphazard and without any objectives. Isolated problems at the whims of the researchers/supervisors are taken up for the study. They have no relevance to the national or regional priorities. They are unconnected and no continuation of the work is done already in that field. Attending relevant seminars would enable the scholars to choose the right guide.

The Sponsoring Agencies

It is not easy task to organize a seminar/workshop without sponsoring agencies. Attending relevant seminars depends upon the sponsoring agencies. Some agencies limit the programme to the academic community and some agencies limit the programme to the field experts only. Now-a-days government agencies like UGC and ICSSR liberally provide financial assistance for the conduct of seminar/workshop at regional, national and international level. Besides, we have research institutions and autonomous institutions like IIM, etc., who sponsor programmes.

At the State level there are plenty of organizations that come forward to sponsor seminar programmes. Now-a-days the commercial banks especially the private sector banks show keen interest in sponsoring the seminar programmes. In our country, the private sector business community is still reluctant to show interest in sponsoring programmes.

There has been no link between the academics and the business institutions at all levels, leave apart the technical institutions like REC, and IIT which are mostly engaged in the independent research activities.

While sponsoring the programmes, there has been a chance to bring together the academy and the business world. This would enable them to find out the practical problems and solutions. The participants should see therefore who are sponsoring agencies and for whom they sponsor so that they could find out whether there is any role for them to play.

We have the following agencies to sponsor and organize seminars/workshops at regular intervals:

National Level

1. The University Grants Commission
2. The Indian Council for Social Science Research
3. All Indian Management Association
4. All Indian Commerce Association
5. Indian Institute of Finance
6. Institute of Company Secretaries of India
7. Institute of chartered Accounts of India
8. Institute of Human Resource Development
9. Research Development Association
10. University
11. Indian Economics Association
12. National Research Development Corporation
13. International Cooperative Alliance
14. National Cooperative Union of India
15. All India Association for Christian Higher Education

State Level

1. District Industries Centre
2. Small Industries Service Institute
3. Commercial Banks

4. Labour/Teachers Association
5. Small Industries Development Corporation
6. National Small Industries Corporation
7. Directorate of Industries and Commerce
8. Colleges
9. Voluntary Association
10. State Cooperative Unions.
11. State Level Federation of Cooperatives

Finance

As how it is difficult to conduct a seminar, it is equally a tough job to attend the seminar. In these days, it is a costly affair. For attending a national seminar, one should spend a minimum of Rs. 3,000, leave a part the delegation fee, boarding and lodging. He has to travel and undergo tedious journey. No organizers are ready to meet these especially for the young scholars. The shortage of funds prevented the participants to attend relevant seminars. Researchers should not therefore mind in spending from their own pocket. However, they would get reward if they sincerely make an attempt to attend the seminars/workshops.

In these days, wise scholar not only attends the seminars, instead they go with research schedule and consult with the subject experts. They are scholars who attend the seminars/workshops. With a number of schedules and get they filled with the help of fellow participants. They go back with the filled schedule. It will be processed and they prepare papers out of it which will be worth for publication. The following shall be the chief objectives of the participants while attending the seminar.

1. It aspires young scholars to develop research bent of mind.
2. Conceive new problems which are relevant to the present day of the society.
3. Enable scholars to apply new tools and methodology.

4. An occasion to share the practical difficulties with the fellow participants.
5. Contact learned scholars and keep in touch with them in the future days.
6. Enable the participants to become full-fledged researchers.

Ask the following questions to get clarified with regard to attending relevant seminar.

I. Why Do We Attend Seminars?

1. To identify the areas to be researched.
2. To test your research findings.
3. To determine the level of acceptance and objectives.
4. To find out the objectives and hypotheses.
5. To decide the objectives and hypotheses.
6. To share your experience.
7. To share others experience.
8. To familiarize with the delegates.
9. To acquaint with the research experts.

II. What Seminar Do We Attend?

1. Seminar which deals with the subjects of national/ regional importance.
2. Seminar to be conducted by the University/Colleges/ Associations.
3. Seminar of your relevant subjects.
4. Seminar that is sponsored by the Government.
5. Seminar that identifies you as a delegate.
6. Seminar conducted by the institutions where you hold membership.

III. When Do You Attend?

1. When you have aspiration for research.

2. When you seek research topics.
3. When you are in the midst of practical difficulties.
4. When you complete your research study.
5. When you want to specialize in a special field.
6. When you are invited to become a resource person.
7. When you need contract with the subject specialists.
8. When your findings give immediate solution.

IV. Where Do You Attend Seminars?

1. At places which are accessible to you.
2. At places where your topic will be discussed.
3. At the places where you meet your colleagues.
4. At the national level seminars organized by the university.
5. At the state level seminars organized by the Government Department.
6. At the regional level seminars organized by the institutions.

V. Whom Do We Contact for the Seminar/Workshop?

1. The organizing body.
2. The Seminar Director/Coordinator/Convener
3. The institutions where you are working.
4. The information centers for collecting secondary data.
5. The agencies for financial assistance.
6. Fellow researchers.
7. www.conferencealerts.com

VI. How to Attend the Seminar/Workshop?

1. Sending your delegate fee and get your name registered.
2. Obtain paper acceptance from the Chairman of the technical session.

3. Prepare an abstract of the paper.
4. Get the copies of the paper for distribution.
5. Move cordially with the fellow participants and give respect to all.
6. Do not think that you know everything.
7. Be punctual.

SECTION – IV

TOOLS OF DATA COLLECTION

16

Preparation of Schedules and Questionnaires

The term "Schedules" and "Questionnaires" are used synonymously by most of the researchers. There is a very thin line of distinction between these terms. It is based on technical distinction. The schedules are those used in personal interviews whereas questionnaires are the forms distributed through mail. This distinction does not seem to have significant bearing on the principle, method and important considerations in preparing the research tools. The methods adopted for preparation of schedules and questionnaires are commonly discussed in this chapter. The questionnaires/ schedule is an indispensable tool in social sciences research. Therefore it has to be scientifically designed. Various steps involved in the preparation of questionnaires (hereafter the term questionnaire will be used to denote both questionnaires and schedules) are discussed below.

Design of the Questionnaire

While planning for the preparation of the questionnaire, the first important aspect to be remembered relating to the questionnaires is who is to answer the questions. It has been said that, "no survey can be better than its questionnaires," which means that however efficient the design or the sampling of the study may be, the success of the survey largely depends on the quality of questionnaires. Moser emphasizes that, "it is fair to say that question design is the survey director's most persistent headache, particularly since it is still so largely a matter of art rather than science. In designing the questionnaire, the guiding principles must be the knowledge of the population, subject matter, common sense, past experience and pilot work. Moser and Kalton advocate the following steps in designing the questionnaire:

1. Define the problems to be tackled by the survey so as to decide on what questions to ask. The temptation is always to cover too much to ask everything that might turn out to be interesting. This must be resisted. Lengthy sampling questionnaires are as demoralizing for the interviewer as for the respondent. The questionnaire should not be longer than is absolutely necessary for the purpose.
2. The survey planning must rigorously examine every question and exclude any that are not strictly relevant to the objectives of the survey. In this respect the pilot survey is the most helpful tool. All the marginal questions can be tested out and dummy tabulations made from the results. Questions likely to prove to be of small importance in the final analysis can be spotted and those which turn out to be not worth asking be excluded.
3. In setting the scope of the questionnaire the questions should be practicable. This needs emphasis, even though no amount of text book admonition can take the place, of common sense. It is no good asking a person's opinion about something he does not understand, about events too distant for him to remember accurately about matters which although they concern him, he is unlikely to have accurate information or that are so personal or emotional that valid answers cannot be expected by formal direct questioning.

Goode and Hatt in their book 'Methods in Social Research', explain the following steps which are necessary at the planning stage:

1. The researcher must learn as much as possible about his subject matter before he begins to formulate questions.
2. The researcher should layout tentatively the logical implications of his problems and then draw upon his own experience and the literature for questions which are relevant to those logical implications. At this point the researcher should consult colleagues to get their thinking on the problem.
3. While the formulation of a list of areas and questions the researcher should submit this list to experts both in the field of the problem and in related fields. With each consultation some changes occur: *(i)* the list of possible questions grows, *(ii)* the number of areas which are of interest increases, *(iii)* the number of areas which the researcher can cover must be decreased, *(iv)* ambiguities, biases, poor phrasing etc. are corrected gradually, and *(v)* a closer logical relationship developed between the parts of the schedule.
4. Any questionnaire must be limited in its length and scope. In general, in the absence of special motivations for the respondent, an interview should not extend much beyond half an hour and even this length is difficult to sustain without fatiguing the informant. Self-administering questionnaires should not, usually require more than 30 minutes to complete and an even shorter period is desirable. Lengthy questionnaire will affect the morale of the interviewer as well as the respondent.

Hence, in planning a questionnaire a researcher must get himself thorough with the subject he has chosen for research. Then he has to decide the areas to be covered by the study and must frame the objectives. The questionnaire areas will ensure the collection of adequate and relevant data. Consultation with experts in the field will also help to prepare an ideal questionnaire.

Unification of Areas

After proper planning is made, major areas of the questionnaire must be arranged in an order to ascertain unification of the areas of the questionnaire. *Goode and Hatt* say that such unification is necessary in order to make the respondent:

(a) Drawn into the interview by awakening his interest

(b) Easily brought along from items which are simple to answer to those which are complex.

(c) Not affronted by an early and sudden request for personal information.

(d) Never asked to give an answer which could be embarrassing without being an opportunity to explain, and

(e) Brought as smoothly as possible from one frame of reference to another rather than made to jump back and forth.

Principles to be Adopted in Organizing the Questions

As for the introductory item of the questionnaire, it should catch the attention of the respondent throughout the interview and should not result in refusals. It is better to avoid controversial items at the beginning. Generally questions are devised in such a way that they have the power to evoke interest and to involve the respondent in the interview without arousing a strong controversial response.

Secondly, simpler items should be introduced in the first and items which require thinking or scratching of the brain or crucial issues must come in the body of the questionnaire. Such questions should not be taken to the end since the interview might have got tired or he might have got interview fatigue. Likewise questions involving too much personal information or delicate questions should not be brought at the beginning.

It is important that sources of embarrassment should be removed from the questionnaire. Questions which are too personal and controversial should be avoided as far as possible.

With regard to the last aspect of moving smoothly from one item to the other, questions pertaining to the same area be placed together so as to have subject sequence. It will also aid the respondent to answer easily.

Question Content

While preparing the questions for the questionnaire the respondent's knowledge of the subject, ability, willingness, etc., must be weighted properly. If we are preparing a questionnaire for educated people we can ask questions with standards or with rich content or what are known as loaded questions. On the other hand, if it is for the uneducated the subject content must be minimum. Moser opines that, "the surveyor should aim to ask questions only from those likely to be able to answer them accurately; to ask about past events only if he can reasonably expect people to remember them accurately and to ask their opinions only if he can be reasonably sure that they understand what is involved and are able to give meaningful answers. It is always well to remember that most survey questions are addressed to a variety of people very differently qualified to answer them.

So much for taking account of the ability of people to give accurate answers, quite as important is their willingness to do so. Except in the rare surveys where people are compelled to give information, there is no formal reason why they must answer survey questions. They generally do so partly due to general helpfulness and partly to their liking to talk about themselves and their views and in part to innocuous nature of the questions themselves.

But willingness is no guarantee that the answers will be accurate. If information is sought on a personal subject about whom people are reluctant to talk, the survey must adopt his interviewing approach accordingly and be prepared to go to some lengths in checking on the accuracy of the responses.

Question Wording or Language

While framing the question the language used must be simple. It must be easily understandable by all the sample respondents. As uniformity in answers are very important for the later stage of processing, the questions must be worded in simple language to give the same meaning to the respondents.

Following are the Principles of Question Making

1. *Use Simple and Familiar Language*

Vocabulary used in the questionnaire should be simple which is used in the daily life. It should be within the comprehension of the least intelligent of the group studied. Phrases and expressions known only in certain regions of the country should be avoided.

2. *Make the Questions Concise*

A question should be as concise as possible, long involved sentences with conditional clauses require extended concentration on the part of the respondent. Such questions confuse the informants and will result in wrong answers. Concise wording and clear arrangement will condense the wide range of information in a small schedule.

3. *Avoid Leading Questions*

Questions and statements of a leading character should be guarded against. According to Moser "a leading is one which by its content, structure of wording, leads the respondent in the direction of a certain answer." For the question: Do you read 'The Hindu Daily?' The respondents tend to answer 'Yes'. Instead the question may be phrased thus: what newspaper do you read daily? Presenting a choice to the respondent is acceptable, provided that more than one choice is offered.

4. Be Specific and Explicit

The question should be made explicit so that the interviewer is able to get the kind of interpretation desired. For example "What kind of radio you own?" may mean anything the model, type of brand. Make the question pin-pointed and specific by giving different alternatives: *(a)* transistor *(b)* trade model; or *(a)* single band *(b)* 2 band *(c)* 3 band; or *(a)* Philips *(b)* Murphy *(c)* Bush *(d)* other (specify).

5. Make the Question Self Explanatory

The question should be self explanatory as far as possible, so that the desired information is gathered and tabulation becomes easy. Questions like where is your birth place? How often do you go to movies? Lack clarity. They should be made more explicit and specific. So also units of enumeration such as rupees, paisas, weights in terms of kgs, and quintals should be clearly defined in the schedule.

6. Avoid Ambiguous Questions

In the question wording ambiguity should be avoided at all costs. Ambiguous question will mean different things to different people. It is confusing and beyond the comprehension of respondents. For example the question: Have you paid back the loan you obtained from the bank? if asked irrespective of the fact whether one obtained the loan or not will be understood differently. A "no" for such question will either mean that one has not obtained loan or one as not paid back the loan. Such ambiguous questions are the result of vague phrasing or unwarranted assumptions.

7. Avoid Vague Questions

Vagueness creeps in the question when the descriptive adjectives and adverbs like good, bad, fair or frequently, occasionally, rarely, are used. Such wording do not have agreed or generally, accepted meaning. Similarly phrases like kind of, 'generally' 'on the whole' etc., should be avoided. For instance; What 'kind of' house be specific such as:

What is the type of roofing in your house? *(a)* Terrace, *(b)* tiled *(c)* thatched?

8. *Allow Maximum Alternatives*

Questions should be phrased in such a way that all possible alternatives are provided. For instance a question regarding marital status of a person should include all the following alternatives: *(a)* single, *(b)* married, *(c)* widowed, *(d)* divorced, *(e)* separated. For questions which have infinite answers, besides, other known answers, 'others-specify' category should be included.

9. *Avoid Double-Barreled Questions*

Each question should cover only one issue. Double-barreled and multiple meaning questions should be split up into two or more questions. Example: Do you think that all the commercial banks in the country should be nationalized and more funds diverted to priority sector?

10. *Avoid Presuming Questions*

Questions should not presume anything about the respondent. For example the question to which party have you voted in the last election? Such question is relevant only after asking a filter question: Did you vote in last election?

11. *Avoid Hypothetical Questions*

Such questions are based on assumptions and predictions. Answers to hypothetical situation will not be realistic, as the respondent never experienced such a situation.

12. *Avoid Questions Which Involve the Prestige*

If an answer to a question is likely to affect the prestige either positively or negatively, such questions will not receive correct answers. People generally want to project a good image of them as generous, progressive and intelligent. A question like do you favour a socialistic a socialistic society, will receive affirmative answer, which may not reflect the inner wishes of the respondent.

13. Avoid Advance Categorization

It is always better to classify the response yourself rather then allowing the respondent to choose the categories. While asking occupation of a respondent advance categorization like, professional, skilled labour, clerks, farmer etc., will affect accuracy. Simply ask, what is your occupation?

Framing of Effective Questions

As pointed out earlier the questions must use simple language and they should be short in nature. Questions can be broken into pieces wherever necessary. Herbert Hyman gives the following criteria in constructing effective questions.

1. Complex questions that require the respondent to go through several steps of reasoning before answering are undesirable and have often resulted in misleading information.
2. Questions on controversial issues should be broken down into components so that the tester can determine the respondents' feeling about many aspects of the problem including those which he refuses to comment upon. A series of specific questions is needed, sometimes referred to as filter-questions in order to gather adequately the reactions to all sides of the issue.
3. When questions feel to assess the degrees of intensity of feeling or conviction, it is often necessary to find out to what extent the respondents' attitude has been crystallized towards the subject. It is well to include a series of "Why" "When" and "How" questions, the answers to which are analyzed in relation to answers to other specific questions.
4. The required answers should be within the informational scope of the respondent.

5. The length of the questions and statement used should be governed by an estimate of the respondents' comprehension level. If a question appears too long, the best way of splitting it should be investigated.

Question Order

While placing various questions in the questionnaire, they should be arranged in proper order. If the questions are not in proper order they may affect the response and the accuracy of the responses may also be affected due to misplacing questions. Improper order of questions may also contradict the responses and the respondent should not be held responsible for such mistakes. Following order should be observed in organizing the questions:

1. Questions asked at the start of the interview should be such that they are easy to answer. Such "stage setting" questions will help to built rapport. They may be factual questions like name, age, occupation or those which appeal to human interest such as fashion, film, etc. It should be ensured that such interest-catching questions are not sensitive and controversial. Advice-seeking questions will also encourage the respondents.
2. Questions should be arranged sequentially according to the subject matter or on the basis of periods. Questions pertaining to one subject or one reference period should be grouped together in order to avoid mental exertion to the respondent.
3. Questions must be arranged logically and must move from one topic to another. The progression of questions should be natural and spontaneous.
4. The transition from one topic to another must be easy and smooth. The questions should not jump abruptly from innocent to embarrassing subjects. While proceeding from one set of questions to another it is better to explain the break and the relevance of a new set of question in one or two sentences.

5. Questions which may embarrass the informant must be placed at the middle of the questionnaire, so that they do not create any misgiving at the close of the interview.
6. Questions which will affect the answer for later questions should not be arranged at the interview.
7. Highly sensitive questions, which may lead to the termination of interview owing to the respondent's refusal to continue the interview, should be placed at the end. If any such refusal is met, the loss of information will be relatively small.

Questions that Need Carefulness

There are certain questions which can be omitted and there are certain questions which need caution while using. Such questions are as follows:

(a) Insufficiently Specific Questions

Questions must be specific to get the expected response. For example, are you satisfied or dissatisfied with your canteen, is unspecific. It must be like this, Are you satisfied or dissatisfied with the prices of meals of your canteen?

(b) Ambiguous Questions

Ambiguous questions are not clear in comprehension. They fall into categories like incomplete references (How well does your mind work over this issue) or indefinite comparisons, of times, place or persons (How often do you go to cinema) Hence, ambiguous questions must be avoided. Vague words and phrases like "fairly" "generally" "many" should be avoided.

(c) Leading Questions

Moser defines a leading question thus: "It is one which by its content, structure or wording, leads the respondent in the direction of a certain answer". For example a question like "Do you read a newspaper like Hindu?" a leading question must also be avoided.

(d) Presuming Questions

Questions should not presume anything about the respondent. It should not imply that he possess that knowledge or have a particular habit. For example ask question "are you a smoker?", only after putting certain filter questions for knowing first he is a smoker.

(e) Hypothetical Questions

Such questions which always attempt to give affirmative answers-would you like an increase in salary? If the response is 'no' there is something wrong. Moser says "If he did (i.e., said no) it could only be because he has taken into account some hidden factors of his own, or because he has failed to".

(f) Personalized Questions

Such questions are those involving too much of personal nature. For example, asking a question on family planning if a question is asked like, "have you undergone Vasectomy?" the answer can be 'no' even from a respondent who had undergone such operation.

(g) Embarrassing Questions

Such questions are those which people do not like to discuss in public. For example questions on family planning for women. To get response to such questions which are very essential female interviewer can elicit response from a women respondent easily.

(h) Questions on Periodical Behaviour

It is about a particular habit like going to cinema, purchases etc. How often do you go to cinema? When did you last go to cinema? Such questions must be asked in a specific and tactful way to get correct response.

(i) Questions Involving Memory

These are questions involving the respondent in

recollecting information—when did you last go to cinema? What was the price paid for paddy in 1976?

(j) Questions Which are too Sensitive

Questions on burning issues such as religion, politics, tradition, superstition etc, should be avoided as far as possible.

(k) Laboured questions

Lengthy questions may involve longer memory of a respondent and to such questions the respondent may get bored or exhausted. For example: some people say walking is good for health some people say cycling is good for health some people say horse riding or swimming is good for health. Which method do you think is good?

Pre-Test

By pre-testing the questionnaire errors can be eliminated, unwanted questions can be removed; language or the wordings can be corrected. *Goode and Hatt* in their book 'Methods in Social Research', give the following advantages of pre-test.

(a) Lack of Order in the Answer

Lack of order in questions may arise if questions do not tap same experience in each respondent. This may be due to the use of difficult words, or questions which attempt to obtain too much data at one time or the other, but whatever the reason may be, totally unordered answers should always lead to critical re-examination of the questions.

(b) "All-or-None Responses"

Such stereo typed responses being answered by all or none must be avoided and the questions must be re-arranged or worded properly.

(c) A High Proportion Don't Know' or Don't Understand Answers'

This is an indication that the questions are improperly drawn or that, a bad sample design has been used. Large percentage of 'don't know' responses suggests that: *(i)* questions are vague, or *(ii)* that they are too complex, or *(iii)* that they involve difficult answers on which the respondent needs expert interviewing help, or *(iv)* that the respondent simply is not in a position to answer the questions.

(d) A Great Number of Qualifications or Irrelevant Comments

Qualifications are the conditions put in answers, i.e., the respondent adds conditions like, 'if' and 'but'. If many of these are offered by the respondents the questions need to be changed or re-arranged.

(e) A High Proportion of Refusals to Answers

During the course of the interview some questions may be unanswered. If the refusal order is above 10 percent, questions need revision. Refusals may be due to the inclusion of a taboo subject without any warning, or a question which is out of context. Refusal may take place if the interviewer asks personal questions which the respondent thinks that he cannot assure anonymity.

17

Mailed Questionnaire

A questionnaire is a tool to collect data from diverse, large and widely scattered social group. Questionnaires are prepared in advance by the interviewer and are generally mailed to the informants. Sometimes questionnaires are also administered to groups. One important factor that differentiates questionnaires and other means of data collection such as interview schedules and interview guides is that the questionnaire is self-administered. The questionnaire will prove to be an effective tool, if used in appropriate research designs and situations. The appropriateness of the mailed questionnaires will depend on: *(i)* the types of information required, *(ii)* the type of respondent reached, *(iii)* the accessibility of respondents, and *(iv)* the precision of the hypothesis.

A great deal of planning and precaution should be exercised before mailing a questionnaire. The mailed questionnaire should not be set abruptly. A covering letter with the needed instructions must be sent along with the questionnaire. The covering letter should be worded in the language known to the respondent. It should also mention the need for the study and under whose auspices the study is conducted. The need for the respondents' cooperation should also be mention in convincing language. The directions to fill up the schedule must also be added, as many of the respondents may be new to such research exposures. Proper direction alone can ensure accuracy of response. Besides impressive preparation of questionnaires, an effective appeal about the significance of the study, guarantee of anonymity of the identity of the respondents are the other rules which should be observed while sending the questionnaire.

Advantages of Mailed Questionnaire

Mailed questionnaire, compared to interview has enormous advantages. It is cheaper and consumers less time, it allows the respondent to express freely. The following are the important advantages of mailed questionnaire.

1. Cheaper in Cost

Mailed questionnaire is cheaper to administer as it involves only postal expenses. Expenses relating to travel by the interviewer are avoided. The problem of supervision is also dispensed with.

2. Covers Larger Area

Mailed questionnaire is very useful to cover a large size of sample. When a study needs to cover the population extending a state or the whole of the country, mailed questionnaire can reach the sample respondents who are far away from the study center.

3. Saving in Time

The use of mailed questionnaire saves the time of respondent as well as that of the researcher. In the absence of the interviewer time taken for unnecessary conversations is saved. Deviations from the main purpose of interview are quite common and such wastage of time is avoided under mailed questionnaire. Moser views that: "It takes little time to send out or to get the bulk of the eventual returns to follow-up attempts. It can be reasonably expected that the mailed questionnaires will be returned within three weeks."

4. Free-Flow of Responses

In the absence of a second party a respondent is allowed to give his responses. He is allowed to take his own time for thinking and to consult and verify information. This can assure free flow of responses.

5. Validity, Reliability and Accuracy

As the respondent is remote from the study center and the absence of personal proximity and association can assure validity of responses. As anonymity is maintained it can safeguard the reliability of the responses. With regard to accuracy Moser and Kalton say that: "mailed questionnaires also have something to commend them when information concerning several members of a household is required. The housewife must be hard put to give accurate figures of the earning of individual members of the household, their average weekly expenditure on meals or even their exact ages and in such situations a mailed questionnaire allowing some 'Intra-household consultation' may lead to more accurate information than a doorstep interview'

6. Problems of Non-Contracts

When a questionnaire is to be administered through interview several respondents may not be available. In villages or rural areas respondents may not be available during the day time as they might have gone to the fields. In cities or urban areas they might have gone to offices. Either early mornings or late evenings must be fixed as the right time for interview. This handicap could be avoided by the mailed questionnaire.

Limitations of Mailed Questionnaire

Mailed questionnaire in spite its merits, falls short of a perfect tool of data collection. Its advantages is centering round the cost. But the greatest drawback of this system is non-response. Further mailed questionnaire has the following limitations:

1. *It Needs Higher Rate of Literacy*

Mailed questionnaire can be used in countries where the rate of literacy is high. Even in countries where the literacy rate is higher, the respondents must have enough knowledge of the subject and implication of research studies. Goode and Hatt warned that, the amount of reading attention and writing skill required most questionnaires is much greater than is implied, by a minimum definition of 'literate'. For many who are able to read and write, neither burden is assumed willingly or easily.

2. *Probing Not Possible*

An interviewer can clarify the responses and can supplement the questions to get clarity in responses by means of a thorough probing. This is not possible with mailed questionnaire. The responses given by the respondent is final. Vague questions, emotional questions, etc., may not be answered well when compared to the interview method.

3. *Response Will Not Be Independent*

As the respondent is allowed to go through the questionnaire he happens to see all the questions before he answers them. This may set a situation to bias answers. Hence, we are not sure that independent answers have been given each question.

4. *Answer by Right Person*

Another limitation with regard to mailed questionnaire is that one is not sure whether the right person fills the questionnaire, in spite of clear instruction. As a result, "the mailed questionnaire is inappropriate where spontaneous answers are wanted; where it is important that the views of one person only are obtained, uninfluenced by discussion with others; and where it is essential that one particular person in each household (say the chief wage-earner) fills in the questionnaire and no one else."

5. Poor Response

Further the rate of response over mailed questionnaire would be poor. Hence, its usefulness for deep studies has been questioned. In countries like India, where the rate of literacy is low and research consciousness even among educated population is at a low level, the usefulness of mailed questionnaire as a tool of data collection raises doubts.

6. Bias

The poor response will lead to sampling bias. The persons who can answer the questions or are willing to answer the questions may be those who are interested in the subject-matter, or those who have higher education or higher socio-economic status. This is a source of bias which will distort the results.

Because of the various limitations, the mailed questionnaire method has very limited applicability. As pointed out by *Goode and Hatt:* "the questionnaire is not an effective research tool for any but a highly select group of respondents." However, if the researcher is cautious in planning and preparation of the project, the non-response could be reduced. The questions that are framed should be simple and must be worded in such a way as to elicit the cooperation of the respondent. As people may often forget things, follow up measures like reminder letter may be resorted. A stamped self-addressed envelop should be enclosed for facilitating easy return of the filled up questionnaires. Such measures will have a healthy impact on the responses for the mailed questionnaires. The non-responses have to be supplemented by personal contract and interview.

18

Interview

Interview is one of the important tools of social research. Interview must be combined with schedule. In other words interview is a technique used to administer the schedule. The person who is interviewing is called as interviewer. An interviewee is called as respondent also. Only through interview, varied types of data can be gathered intensively and extensively. Besides, interview is a means for assessing the personality of the respondent.

Young defines interview as "an effective informal verbal and non-verbal conversation, initiated for specific purposes and focused on certain planned areas."

Objectives of Interview

The main purpose of interview as a research is tool to gather data extensively and intensively. It also helps to measure the personality of the respondent. It provides an opportunity for the interviewer to move freely with the respondents and to study their reaction to particular questions. Pauline Young spells out the following objectives of interview. The objectives of interview may be exchange of ideas and experiences, eliciting of information pertaining to a wide range of data in which the interviewee may wish to rehearse his future possibilities. As the very term implies interviewing is an interaction process. It is a mutual view of each of the other.

The objectives of interview are:

1. To exchanges ideas and experiences
2. To elicit information

Advantages of Interview

As a tool of data collection, the interview has certain specific advantages. They are as follows:

1. Measuring Personality

To assess the personality of the respondents it is a very useful tool. Emotions, opinions, reactions etc. are measured by means of taking the respondent to various issues. Such measurement of personality is not possible in tools like questionnaire.

2. Full Information Collected

By means of an interview, all information and data needed for the study are collected. Interview leads to probing an interviewee which further gives full scope to elicit detailed information. The interviewer can ask additional questions not enumerated in the schedule. By this process, clarity and continuity of responses are attained. The interviewer has also the freedom to clarify the questions. It is through this manual process, smooth responses are achieved.

3. Delay Due to Non-Response Avoided

In the other methods, especially in the mailed questionnaire method lot of time is consumed to complete the process of data collection. The rate of response will also be sometimes poor. These limitations are all avoided by interview method because proper rapport is created before starting the interview.

4. *Accuracy of Responses*

The interviewer can eliminate unwanted responses. Thus, he can record only the needed responses. Accuracy of responses is arrived at by means of asking questions under conducive climate, by means of probing and by means of asking additions and clarifying the questions of the respondent.

Qualities of an Interviewer

The interviewer who is undertaking the task of meeting various respondents must have certain qualities. Basically the interviewer must have enough knowledge about the subject and must be familiar with the research techniques. He must have got adequate training in the field of survey research. Eminent research authorities all agree on the following qualities needed for an interviewer.

1. *Honesty*

Honesty denotes the straight forwardness and truthfulness to the duty of data collection. Even without meeting the respondents one may be tempted to fill up the schedule, based on previous interviews. It is said that, "Honesty and integrity are not characteristics that can be easily assessed at the selection stage, but interviewer who are later found deficient on these scores can and should be quickly dismissed."

2. *Interest*

The interviewer must have enough aptitude for this type of job. He should not consider it as an unattractive job or a stop-gap arrangement to further his career. Moser stresses that, "errors and poor quality of work are much more likely if the interview is bored and regards the work as valueless. The quality of most interviewer's work deteriorates after a time an important consideration to remember when they are being engaged for a lengthy period."

3. *Accuracy*

Interviewers should be accurate in their recording of answers. They should scrupulously follow instructions, and faithfully carry out their administrative duties.

4. *Adaptability*

The interview must adapt himself to different types of surveys, respondents, places, and time. He should not have any bias and prejudice against certain groups of the population.

5. *Personality and Temperament*

An interviewer must avoid 'over-rapport, with the respondent. He should not involve himself emotionally with the respondent. "Interviewing on most surveys is a fairly straight forward job, not one calling for exceptional industry charm or tact. What one asks is that the interviewer's personality should be neither over-aggressive nor over-sociable. Pleasantness and a business-like manner is the ideal combination."

6. *Intelligence and Education*

The interviewer must have sufficient education and intelligence to follow the instructions given to him to conduct the interview.

Limitations of Interview

Interview has the following limitations:

1. *Interviewer Bias*

An interviewer may have bias relating to the socio-economic activities. He may have leaning towards certain ideologies. The interviewer may approach the respondent with a set of beliefs and pre-conceived notions. Such biases may be reflected while interviewing as well as in recording the responses.

2. *Forgetfulness*

Sometimes the interviewer may forget to record the data or he may record irrelevant facts omitting the relevant. He has to grasp the response carefully and must record the needed responses. This he may fail due to faulty memory, or lack of insight. Ralph Berdie, who has made an extensive study of the psychological elements in interviewing found that, because memory and retention are highly selective processes, interviewees under proper circumstances generally gave accurate and vivid accounts of the most recent or the most intense experiences or of the situations which they encountered most frequently.

3. *Meeting of Minds*

In very many circumstances the interviewer and the respondent will never come to a common place of thinking. It is possible that each one will be emphasizing his own position forgetting the course of interview. It is not uncommon for the interviewer to drag the respondent on certain issues or controversies. The chances of such controversy are all the great when the interviewer and the interviewee hail from different social backgrounds with different ideologies and values. Under such circumstances there is every likelihood of clash of ideas irreconcilably which will seriously affect the utility of data.

4. *Subjectivity*

Lack of objectivity in approaching the interviewee is a common drawback of interviewer. The interviewee sidesteps his experiences and may focus his attention towards issues not relevant to the subject. The same thing may be repeated by the interviewer. *Young* says that, "at times the interviewer holds rigidly to his objectives and is not sensitive to the value of the bypaths radiating out from the main scheme of his formulated plan. When he drives hard towards his own objectives, he tends to inject his own personal goal and may fail to see that of his subject."

5. *Impact of Emotions*

Interviewers as well as the interviewee are human beings and they are susceptible to the impact of emotions like any other human beings. At the time of interview the respondent or the interviewer might have heard shocking information or might be facing family problems or had travel weariness. Such circumstances may certainly influence the normal response or normal interview.

Steps Involved in the Interview

Before starting an interview the interviewer as well as the research authorities must prepare all arrangements to conduct the interview and to bring out the positive effects. Rapport is an important aspect of interview and before starting the interview the interviewer must familiarize to the respondent. The other steps involved in the interview are as follows:

1. *Planning and Preparation*

Careful planning and meticulous preparations are necessary to make an interview successful. In the case of structured interview, interview guide must be at the disposal of the interviewer. John Best emphasizes that the preparation for the interview is a critical step in the procedure. The interviewer must have a clear conception of just what information he needs. He must clearly outline the best sequence of questions and offer stimulating comments that will systematically bring out the desired responses. A written down outline, schedule or check list will provide a set plan for the interview precluding the possibilities that the interviewer will fail to get important and needed data.

While planning an interview, it is necessary to take proper introduction letters. Young advices, that the introduction should if at all possible, be personal or by one who in a sense sponsors the interviewer. This will not only make the respondent trust the interviewer but also make him willingly cooperate with the interviewer.

It is often advised by experts that the interviewer must contact the leaders of the village or community to get the cooperation of the respondents. Introduction of the interviewer by such leaders will be more effective than direct contact of the respondents.

Young insists that when studying a community or a cultural group it is often wise to interview the leaders first, to enlist their cooperation, and if they see any justification for the study to have them recommended the interviewer to others in the group. Goode and Hatt hold the same view. They say that when the interviewer has a list of specific respondents whom he must interview personally, his first contact is not with the interviewee but with a member of the family or a friend. In these cases he must remember that the people must be understood as well, if he is to persuade the respondent to give the interview.

2. *Starting the Interview*

After careful initial planning and meeting the leaders or heads of households, the interviewer can approach the respondent for the interview. Before starting the interview as such or coming to the business he must inform the interviewer of his purpose of conducting the interview. Such aspect is called as rapport. The need to create such contact is pointed out by Young as follows: He is entitled to know why he is being interviewed particularly since a considerable expenditure of his time and energy may be involved. Cooperation can be enlisted by asking for help in the study under way. To have good rapport, the interviewer must take the respondent in his confidence. Even if the circumstances are unfavourable, a skilled interviewer need not be disappointed. Moser observes that, "the form of the interview opening is nevertheless crucial to win those who are less willing to cooperate. The time may be inconvenient; the subject of the survey may be antagonistic towards surveys in general. Then it is that the interviews and also the researcher's attitude counts......it should be the interviewers duty to explain why and for whom, the survey is being done, what is expected to emerge from it, to whom the results will be of interest and so on...."

While doing so, the interviewer should be honest and avoid exaggerating the benefits expected of the survey; nor should he give false promises. Besides he should be polite and ask for the information pleasantly. Such a human relation approach will induce the people to cooperate even when they are not convinced about the utility of the survey.

It is also necessary to inform the respondent of the confidential nature of the data collected. They should be assured that their name will not be revealed at any time and the data collected are used purely for research purpose and without any ulterior motives. These things can ensure a bond between the interviewer and interviewees. The interviewer should not stop with mere creating the rapport. He must come to his business slowly.

Creating rapport is only an element which paves way for beginning the interview in a conducive atmosphere and it is not an end by itself. The interview is far from being a mere personal friendly conversation. It is a conversation with a purpose. The interviewer should slowly come to his business and maintain professional competence. He should not lose himself in being friendly, best he can neither command respect nor do justice to the task he is performing. He must be courteous and at the same time business like. His talk should have the warmth and personal exchange of a conversation, with the clarity and guidelines of a scientific search.

The interview must be carried on in an informal conversational style. Even where there is a structured schedule they have to be asked conversationally rather than read stiffly. During the conversation the interviewer must listen to the words of the respondent. In other words, the interviewer should not interfere unnecessarily. *Young* points out that "When an interviewee feels that he will not meet with interruptions, denial, contradictions and other harassments, he is not likely to resist and withhold information. People are motivated to communicate when the atmosphere is permissive, the attitude non-judgmental, when the listener is so genuinely absorbed in the revelations that he can identify himself at least vicariously, and gain sympathetic insight.'

3. *Asking the Questions*

Unless the interview is of non-structured type, the interviewer must ask each question exactly as it is worded. Each question must be carefully pre-tested, to express the precise meaning desired in as simple a manner as possible. Even a slight reordering of a questions other than those specifically authorized in the instructions should be carefully avoided. Such an explanation may change the frame of reference and bias the response. If each interviewer is permitted to vary interview questions as he likes, there will be no way of comparing responses. Hence, an interviewer can repeat the questions slowly with a proper emphasis offering only such explanation as are given in the instructions.

The question should also be asked in the same order as they appear on the schedule. Each questions sets up a frame of reference for succeeding questions and if the order is changed responses may not be in order as required. *Moser* cautions that, "they are expected to ask all the applicable questions, to ask them in the order given and with no more elucidation and probing than is explicitly allowed, and to make no unauthorized variations in the wording." *Goode and Hatt* also emphasized that "if a man's emotions seem fairly strong, the interviewer might well smile and wait in interested silence, encouraging the respondent to talk out his annoyance. Then the question should be simply repeated and in most situations it does not need to be rephrased at all."

The interviewer must ask all questions on the schedule unless there are instructions to skip over certain questions. In certain cases a question to be asked might have been answered previously as a side comment on an earlier question. Such a question should be repeated in order to get direct answer or an entirely different answer, than the earlier answer.

Goode and Hatt in their book, "Methods in Social Research", broadly suggests the following instructions while asking questions:-

1. The interviewer cannot be a passive listener. He must be a critical and intelligent questioner.
2. The interviewer must use his ingenuity to avoid losing the interview. He must probe more deeply to avoid the clichés which are used to cover motivations.
3. The interviewer cannot be satisfied with merely writing down the answer. He must be certain that he understands the answer and that is actually an answer to question. Often this will require further questioning, an attempt to probe more deeply into the meaning of the response given.
4. When the respondent does not have the information, a probe will be of no use, except to be certain that the respondent really does not know.
5. If there is a large percentage of 'don't know' answers to a given question, it means that the question itself is not properly phrased. In such cases, it is necessary to discover the communication problem and to rephrase the question in the draft of the schedule so as to elicit a greater proportion of answers.

Pauline Young in her book "Scientific Social Surveys and Research" suggested the following methods of questions.

1. Questions must be not only timely and wisely rationed but they must also be phrased in terms that show concern to the interviewee's problem.
2. It may be assumed that if information does not supply definite answers to direct questions, the chances are, he will do so to indirect questions. Indirection may be used to resolve resistances.
3. It should always be kept in mind that the interview period belongs to the interviewee. It is his moment and it may have been preceded by moments of long anxious waiting to talk and be listened to.
4. Once the interviewee narrates his account of past or present events, the interviewer must watch every term for validity and consistency of the account without interfering with unwarranted questions.

5. Double question though deemed related to each other should be avoided as they are often confusing.
6. Questions tending to bring forth short, unrevealing replies or 'Yes' or 'No' response should be avoided. Instead of asking 'Do you know about....? Question should be "what do you know about...?"
7. It may become necessary to control the course of the interview to some extent. Although always on the alert to discover important bypaths, the interviewer may find it essential to check the flow of the story, to harp back to the point of the departure and encourage an interviewee to retrace a line of thought.
8. When interviewees take exception or raise objections to something the interviewees say, implies, or stands for, it is best not to defend oneself. By so doing the interviewer may land himself in a controversy. He may have to clarify his position in order to avoid misunderstanding. Often, silence and inconspicuous change of subject matter may be the most effective way of avoiding argument.

4. *Eliciting Complete Response*

Obtaining clear and complete response to questions is an important, at the same time a difficult aspect of interview. People may simply respond: 'Don't know' to questions, in order to avoid thinking or to evade real answers. Interviewers may misinterpret the question and may give a wrong answer; sometimes he may contradict himself. The interviewer should be alert of all such situations and must elicit complete and correct responses. Simple repetition may sometimes help to get a complete answer.

Kahn and Cannell distinguish five principal symptoms of inadequate response. They are:

(a) *Partial response:* In which the respondent gives a relevant but incomplete answer.

(b) *Non-response:* When the respondent remains silent or refuses to answer the question.

(c) *Irrelevant response:* In which the respondent does not answer the question asked.

(d) *Inaccurate response:* When the question is answered by a reply which is biased or distorted.

(e) *Verbalized response problem:* When the respondent explains why he cannot answer the questions, perhaps because he fails to understand it, because he lacks in the information necessary for answering it, or because he thinks it is irrelevant or inappropriate.

In order to elicit full information the interviewer should explain the question to make sure that the respondent understands it fully. If the answer is found inadequate, the interviewer can stimulate the respondent for further explanation. However the interviewer should ensure that such explanations do not affect the standardization of the questions. Sometimes mere repetition of the question will be sufficient to convey the full meaning. A brief pause and expectant glances indicating that something more is required may have good effect; but the same when overdone will have negative effect. Encouraging words, appreciative phrases like, 'I see', 'That is correct', etc., will convey to the respondent the sympathetic interest the interviewer has in the problem as well as the person.

Probing is an essential item to elicit full answers. If the respondents' answers are vague or too general or incomplete the interviewer has to resort to probing. Probing is needed in order to ascertain the accuracy of the answers given. Only by probing, an interviewer can avoid 'don't know' answers as well as vague and ambiguous answers. It is a request for either repeating the question if it is not properly understood; or for further information and explanation if there is any gap in the answer given. For effective probing the interviewer needs special training and skill.

5. Recording the Interview

Recording the interview is one of the important functions of an interviewer. This is a difficult task and the fruits of labour lie with proper recording of responses. Goode and Hatt advice that "the exact words of the respondent should be recorded. They should not be edited for grammar or meaning. Since most interviewers will not have a command of shorthand, it is necessary to develop skill in writing fast and legibly with some attention to symbols for common short phrases such as "of the" also, or words common in the particular researcher study."

The answers of the respondent are to be recorded differently in the case of pre-coded questions and open ended questions. In the pre-coded questions it is enough if the interviewer makes tick over the relevant answer. In the case of open-ended questions he has to use his skill, rationality and expertise. In this case while recording the answers the meaning of the response should not be misrepresented by wrong recording. As far as possible the exact words of the respondents must be recorded. Errors may arise in both type of questions, due to the following factors:

(a) weariness due to travel and walk before reaching the respondent,

(b) repetitively administering lengthy questionnaires to several respondents,

(c) psychological upset caused by ill-tempered, non cooperative respondents,

(d) simultaneous operation of asking questions, recording, verifying the correctness and preparing for asking next question.

In the course of the interesting conversation, there is always a possibility that the interviewer may forget, to record the responses. He might even be thinking that he has recorded the responses. To avoid such error, the interviewer himself can check the completeness of data collected. If possible mechanical aids like tape recorders can be used. In case of open ended questions, immediate recording of the response will be helpful or after the interview is over, the interviewer can record the incomplete answers. It is also suggested that, the interviewer may make it a practice to go directly from the interview to a type writer or desk, in order to write out the details while the materials are still fresh in his mind. Even under such circumstances, memories can be treacherous, and delay of any proportions may quickly distort or blur the details. The comments which seemed so clear during the interview begin to lose their distinctness and the "why and wherefores" offered by the respondent lose their reasonable quality. The comments which are scribbled in haste during an intensive probing, should be immediately transformed into detailed notes while the experience is still afresh and vivid in the interviewer's memory.

6. *Closing the Interview*

While closing the interview, the interviewer must check whether he has collected all the information needed, completeness of data attained, clarifications properly recorded and has not omitted to ask a question or forgotten to code an answer. Closing an interview is as important as the starting an interview. It must be natural and it should not be closed in a hurry. The naturalness of the climate prevailing at the beginning must also prevail while closing the interview. It is the responsibility of the interviewer to see that the interview is closed at a right time without undue strain. Goode and Hatt advise that "for the qualitative interview, of longer duration and great intensity, the interviewer will have to select his occasion for departure more carefully."

The interviewer after closing the interview can engage in a conversation other than the interview subject. But he must be careful in not leading the respondent to a controversy. The time at his disposal is short and he must indicate his position to leave the respondent and to proceed to his work further. Such situation has been explained better by *Goode and Hatt* in the following words: "Although his departure should not be abrupt, it can atleast be deliberate open and continuous. Assembling his papers for a final check asking a further question to be certain of a previous answer. Putting the papers in a folder or clip board, even while continuing the conversation, allows the situation to be defined as one of leave-taking. This restricting of the situation sets the stage for a final handshake, a thank you and a good-bye."

While taking leave the interviewer should do well to express thanks in recognition of the respondent's cooperation. Generally the parting should be pleasant and mutually satisfying.

19

Observation

Observation is a primary tool of scientific enquiry. It is increasingly employed in social science research as in physical or natural science researches. For instance the anthropologists observe the activities, folk ways, modes of tribal-people, psychologists observe the psychological behaviour of infants and adults, sociologists observe various aspects of a community, and educationists observe the social situation, teacher pupil interaction within the class room and teacher effectiveness. The list is not exhaustive. It could be extended to athletic coaches who observe the performance of the teams in inter-school competition and also cooperative experts who observe the democracy in action in general body meetings. The observation technique is perhaps the only logical approach available for the study of complex social problems. Observation gives an opportunity for direct first hand knowledge and authentic picture about the social phenomena. But it must be clearly understood that it is supplementary to other methods and techniques of scientific enquiries as it is sometimes only through direct observation certain types of data/information can be obtained.

What is Observation?

Observation means acquiring knowledge through the use

of sense organs. In the strict sense, it implies the use of eyes rather than the ears and the voice. Observation is not merely seeing things or activities or situations. It is watching minutely, slowly and systematically the occurrences with a purpose in a given situation with a view to deriving the results. *The Oxford Concise Dictionary* defines observations as, accurate watching and noting of phenomena as they occur in nature with regard to cause and effect or mutual relations. *Dr. P.V. Young* defines observation as "a systematic and deliberate study through the eye of spontaneous occurrences at the time they occur." According to *Goode and Hatt*, "observation includes the most casual uncontrolled experiences as well as the most exact film records of laboratory experimentation." The purpose of observation is to perceive the nature and extent of significant interrelated elements within the complex social phenomena, culture patterns or human conduct. Observation seeks to ascertain the external behaviour of persons in a variety of situations controlled or uncontrolled. It becomes a scientific technique to the extent that it,

(i) serves a formulated research purpose,

(ii) is planned systematically,

(iii) is recorded systematically and related to more general propositions rather than being presented as a set of interesting curiosity, and

(iv) is subjected to checks and controls on validity and reliability. Therefore, as a research technique observation should be expert, purposive, systematic, carefully focused and thoroughly recorded and it should also be accurate, valid and reliable.

Observation has three important components namely, *(a)* sensation *(b)* attention and *(c)* perception.

(a) Sensation gained through the sense organs. Man has six senses, i.e., sight, hearing, touch, smell, taste and rationality. Some of these senses work in combination and our response may be a result of this combination. The eye is a much specialized organ through which we see and understand what happens around us. As stated by Dr. M.H. Gopal the reliability and fullness of the sensory reactions to the situation depend on how keen the sensory organs are and therefore the researcher should be physically in top condition and it is the personality of the observer that makes for accurate observation.

(b) The second element in observation is attention. By attention we mean the process by which a certain small area of the conscious field is focused on. In other words, it implies the researcher's ability to concentrate on the subject under study. Interest, motivation, novelty, inner drives, will power, adequate training and experience etc., are the contributing factors for concentration.

(c) The third ingredient, perception means interpretation of the sensory reports. It is a complex of sensory and imagine elements. "Perception is always a built-up complex experience out of sense impressions, characteristics and qualities supplied by mental activities." In other words, the activity of the organism in converting a sense impression into awareness of an object or meaningful situation is called the process of perception. As pointed out by Dr. M.H. Gopal a sensation merely reports the facts by grouping and identifying sensations. The factors which determine perception are figure and proximity of the object, similarity or likeness, familiarity or post experience, imagination and thought.

Characteristics of Observation

The general characteristics of observation are discussed below:

1. Observation is a physical as well as mental activity. In every act of scientific observation the sense faculties are involved. Observation has three distinguishable components namely sensation, attention and perception.
2. Observation is always specific and selective. It is

not just seeing any thing and everything. It is carefully defining things and the act of observation is narrowed down.

3. Observation is purposive and not random. It is guided by distinct motives or gainful purposes. It may be done to study the complex social problems or measurement of personality or characteristics or studying the complex behaviour of people.
4. Observation is systematic and scientific. What to observe, how to observe, when to observe, whom to observe and where to observe etc. are clearly defined and carefully planned. Intelligent planning, expert execution adequate recording and scientific interpretation are various steps involved in a scientific and systematic observation.
5. Observation is exerted, that is done by a specially well-trained person for a distinct purpose. To make the observation efficient and more accurate the investigator should be thoroughly conversant with the problem under investigation. He should possess the necessary skills to understand and analyze the complex social problems and situations. He must have the ability to estimate and discriminate the valid and invalid results. The observer should be well-versed in the use of observation and recording devices and techniques. Further, he must have sound sense organs, alertness, and good physical condition. He should be unbiased and impartial, besides being free from superstitious beliefs, conservatism, prejudice, etc.
6. "Observation is quantitative usually with a tally of the number of instances a particular type of behaviour has occurred; sometimes total duration of the particular conduct during the period of observation or the distance traveled by a child, or some other countable or measurable characteristic, sometimes a diagram is made showing spatial relationships."

7. A record is made of the observation as promptly as possible. All occurrences have to be carefully noted either at the time of observation or immediately after the observation. The social investigator uses recording devices such as check lists, rating scales, score cards, sealed specimens and blank forms for tallying frequencies. The use of well constructed performs of the above listed, helps in summarizing and quantifying of the data collected by observation.
8. The results of all systematic observation are subjected to checks and verification. The results are checked and substantiated by comparing the results of different observers or by repeating the study to ascertain reliability and validity.

Choice of Observational Technique

In social science, the choice of observational technique is a very important aspect to be considered. The choice naturally depends on the nature and purpose of the study. Whatever may be the purpose of the study, the observer must be sure about the following points: *(a)* What should be observed? *(b)* How observations should be conducted? *(c)* What are the aids to be used? *(d)* How should observations be recorded? *(e)* How to ensure reliability of data? *(f)* What relationship should exist between the observer and the observed and how can such a relationship be established?

The scientific observation may be classified as follows:

1. Participant and non-participant observation
2. Controlled and non-controlled observation
3. Structured and unstructured.

1(a) Participant Observation

Observation may be: *(a)* participant or *(b)* non-participant. These concepts were first introduced in social science by Prof. Edward C. Lindeman. He suggested that if one was interested to know what the subject was really doing; one should watch him and not ask him. The French social reformer by name Frederick Le Play and the English reformer Charles Booth, used this technique in their famous social surveys in 1886. Prof. Le Play who used the participant observation technique in his study entitled *European Working Class Families*, stated that the investigators lived as members of the family as participants in community activities, taking part in games and dances and in study but did not disclose that their purpose was to gather facts.

Another appropriate example of participant observation could be traced in the writings of Verrier Elwin, who gained rare insights into the lives of Gonds and the Nagas. Elwin, an Englishman who come to India was interested in the life and activities of the tribes of India. He lived many years in the Chota-Nagpur area, married a Gond lady and lived with the tribes. Later, he spent many years in Nagaland and undertook intensive studies of the Nagas and other tribes in that area. His research report provides us valuable information about the tribes in India.

Dr. W.T.V. Adiseshiah, one of the leading psychologists in India defined participant observation as any act of observation undertaken in circumstances which include the observer as a part of the things or surroundings which he is observing. Goode and Hatt have pointed out that in participant observation the investigator may play the role of a visiting stranger, an attentive listener, an eager learner or as complete participant observer, registering, recording and interpreting behaviour of the group.

As is evident by the name, in participant observation, the investigator lives with the participants/group for a given period of time as a member of the group. Further, he shares the life and activities of the community, observing, what is going on around him but supplementing this by conversations, interviews and studies of records. Through some degree of participation, in the life of a group is indispensable for a participant observation. The observer need not carry out the same activities as others in order to be a participant observer. He may attempt to find some other role which is acceptable to the group and at the same time does not affect the usual patterns of behaviour.

A participant observer is interested to gain greater insight into the activities. His intimate and active participation helps to penetrate into the thoughts, emotions and actions of the group. His closer contract with the field situation avoids misleading meaningless questions and provides him with a variety of useful information which cannot otherwise be gathered but only through formal methods of investigation. Participant observation also facilitates the sensing and the learning of the social atmosphere the inter-relations between members and the group. Further, participant observation has its psychological values; "it often tends to accustom the group to the observer and at times even to accept him and incorporate him more or less as a member." Participant observation is thus more reliable, flexible and extremely searching. It also discloses the minute, delicate and hidden facts.

The successful role of the observer in studying the life of a community as whole depends on: *(i)* the nature and size of the community; *(ii)* the practical demands of the situation; *(iii)* what the observer wishes to observe; *(iv)* his adaptability, and *(v)* his own personality and skill. If the community is small and closed, say a family, the researcher may live with it and share in its activities, but cannot become a full member of it and remain to certain extent an outsider. Further, if the observer is accepted by the community/ group for practical purpose as one of themselves the observer will get more authentic picture of their behaviour as they may feel free to express their ideas and thus the observer can record the natural behaviour of the group.

It is very important that the observer should not associate too closely with one particular group in the community he is studying. He should enter into the life of a community at several different levels so as to get a complete or a whole picture. Sometimes his closeness may be instrumental in affecting changes in the group behaviour. Therefore, one should be careful in his total immersion. As pointed out by Dr. W.T.V. Adiseshiah, the participant observer should avoid becoming a kind of spy on the group which he observes. The feeling that one is being spied upon creates a feeling of insecurity and an attitude of hostility towards the observer. The participant observer should remember that he has to gather a spontaneous and unopposed picture of the participant and therefore he should be patient and unhurried. He should be imaginative and willing to spend long hours pain-staking in search of truth. Further he should not emotionally get involved in the group.

The success of the participant observation ultimately depends on his skill, personality, how he introduces himself to the community/group and how good a relationship builds up with its members. That it is rightly observed "that participant observation is a highly individual technique."

1(b) Non-Participant Observation

Non-participant observation takes place when some activity is in progress and the observer keeps himself outside that activity and records what is going on. Observation may be of a non-participant type, when observing and recording conditions in a classroom, in a superintendent's or principal's office, in slums, factories, retail stores, banks, strikes, ceremonies and rituals, police station, judicial courts or mayor's office.

Non-participant observation has been compared to snapshots by a busy tourist rather than a studio photograph. It lacks to a great extent, accurate study of the situation as the scope for penetration into the activities is very much limited. This does not mean that non-participant observation is not scientifically useful or desirable. Eminent writer on the subject like *Dr. P.V. Young* says that "even external and scattered observations, much like a series of snapshots by a busy tourist, often suggest the inner life of the people, the human passions which ebb and flow in their group, their conflicts, and social distances. External observations pave the way for a more systematic study of forces influencing social life."

In all social investigations, participant observation may not be a desirable method or it is almost impossible for the outsider to be a genuine participant. For example a social scientist cannot become a criminal in order to study a criminal gang. So also he cannot be a true member of a juvenile gag, a police squad etc. In such cases non-participant observation is the best method.

The non-participant observation has the merit of maintaining objectivity and scientific outlook. The observer can be unattached and impartial which enable him to command the respect and cooperation from everyone in the group. The group may also be willing to disclose even their weakness or delicate matters to the observer since he has more opportunities to conduct formal interviews with the members. It is also claimed that non-participant observation can be easily checked, verified or repeated by another person.

In modern researches, both the participant and non-participant methods are combined with a view to gaining the advantages of the two systems. For example, Robert K. Merton in his housing study used both participant and non-participant methods. The research team developed a careful plan for dual entry into the community, privately at the higher administrative level of the housing project manager and publicly at the level of community organizations and avoided the problem of being identified with the manager, while obtaining the official permission which was necessary for effective field work. In order to study cooperative democracy in action, we may not only get data from various sources such as Acts and Rules of cooperative societies, minutes book, bylaws, audit reports, annual reports, office-bearers, officials but also we may attend the general body and board meetings by creating suitable occasion for observation. Further, if we want to conduct a survey among school children to ascertain their behaviour pattern and living conditions, we can use both participant and non-participant methods to arrive at fruitful findings. Similar combination has been tried in a number of cases in recent years.

2(a) Non-Controlled Observation

In social science research, most of the data that we derive are from non-controlled observation, whether participant or non-participant. We learn the social behaviour from the situations which we have witnessed or participated. The life situations are such as can hardly provide the chance of laboratory method of study. Therefore, they have to be observed in natural surroundings where they occur. As *Dr. P. V. Young* has rightly pointed out "Life situations which can be adequately studied under controlled and artificial conditions are relatively few. Often we have to observe while the observing is good and in the exact social and cultural setting in which the situations occurred."

According to *Dr. M.H. Gopal* "Non-controlled observation is characterized by the absence of any attempt to use precision instruments to measure and record facts and to check their accuracy". Thus, in non-controlled observation the investigator visits the place of occurrence of phenomena. The participant observer using non-controlled observation lives or shares in the life of the group which he is studying. No attempt is made to measure anything but merely to obtain a spontaneous and unopposed picture of individuals. Data are collected without standardizing procedure and without resorting to a random sampling. It may be recalled that social scientists like Charles Booth, William F. Whyte and Nels Anderson used non-controlled observation in their famous studies long-ago. It was reported that these studies provided them with sources of information which could not be gathered otherwise.

Non-controlled observation provides us valuable preliminary data, while helping in the development of mere precise observations which should occupy a later phases of investigation. But it is often said that non-controlled observation is not reliable, because one may be tempted to generalize from stray incidents without properly verifying them. Observation may also be biased by the view of the observer as there is no check upon him. Further, the investigator enters in the field situation thinking that he knows more than what he actually observes. In practice, therefore non-controlled observation is supplemented by schedules of information. Goode and Hatt also suggest that "Informal methods may be supplemented by highly structured observation by detailed questionnaire and by psychological or sociological tests. Thus, what the sociologist or social anthropologist does in an unsystematic fashion, in order to arrive at any conclusions at all, can be carried out by more reliable procedures."

2(b) Controlled Observation

Controlled observation is not very uncommon in social science research. This technique has been introduced in social science to rectify the defects that are noticed in uncontrolled observation. Not only that, as our ideas, in-depth and sharpness, but also we wish to rely on much less uncontrolled observation. In the filed of education, psychology, management science, cooperation and physical education, etc., there is much scope for the application of this technique. In the early period of thirties some valuable and in-depth studies were conducted in the field of child behaviour based on this technique. Dr. Dorothy S. Thomas (1933) for example, conducted some studies on nursery school children. This study was primarily concerned with the social behaviour and reaction patterns of nursery school children to a multiplicity of stimuli encountered experimentation were done in the Iowa Child Welfare Research Station at the University of Iowa (U.S.A.) in the areas of nutrition, physical growth, child psychology, pre-school education, character education and the relative influence of nature versus nature in intellectual development etc.

Dr. W.T.V. Adiseshiah defines controlled observation as observation undertaken with due regard for accuracy and trust worthiness of the evidence collected by applying tools of research. In other words, controlled observation is meant for gathering formalized and customized data using measuring devices as aids to accuracy and standardization. In is usually made according to definite and pre-arranged research plans.

In recent years controlled observation has become a useful method for studying small groups. Controlled observation can be applied to describe the behaviour of conference leaders, behaviour of children in a variety of situation, the administrative efficiency of a social institution, the record of personal behaviour or the characteristics of social groups in a community etc. Similarly, studies can also be conducted to find out the effect of lighting upon production in factories.

Ways of Control

Controlled observation may take place in natural and laboratory situations. We can exercise control in two ways: *(i)* control over the phenomena, and *(ii)* control over the observer. The phenomena may be put to laboratory test under guided controlled conditions. In laboratory situations, the controls are applied to both observer and observed. But, it is difficult for a social science researcher to control the object under study; however he can very well control himself. Goode and Hatt observed: "Control can be applied to the observer by controlling the situation itself, by restricting or defining carefully the participation of the observer by the use of precise categories, observation schedules and other standardized tools for observation and the keeping of records." It must be noted that a variety of control devices are used for pointed, objective and standardized observation. They are carefully drawn schedules, or questionnaires, observation records, attitude scales, field notes, photographs, maps socio-metric scales, motion pictures, sound recorders, films, etc. Mechanical devices help to reproduce the same phenomena at any time and study it objectively. Motion pictures are used in the study of physical activities and sports such as gymnasium performances, observing the moment of the players of foot-ball, basket ball, base ball, tract events etc. Dr. Charlotte Buhler, a clinical psychologist of Los Angeles General Hospital (U.S.A.), conducted a successful study using mechanical devices in the observation of young school children. In her study she was more concerned about the whole personality of the child-sense perceptions, social reactions and mental productivity i.e., means of reasoning and mental initiative. She also observes the children's behaviour in certain test situations—child's free drawing, child's activities and attitudes when playing with a doll.

Controlled observation helps to achieve grater precision and objectivity. It is also possible to check any bias due to the influence of external factors or inadequate data. *Goode and Hatt* pointed out that 'systematic observation limits the bias of the individual observer partly by making the subjects feel the situation as natural but far more through the application of controls on the observer in the form of mechanical synchronizing devices, formulation of hypotheses, team observation, films and recording schedules and inventories." Further, they stated that guesses about distance can be corrected by exact maps. Casual hunches about friendship patterns can be checked by definite counts, cross tabulations or socio-metric diagrams.

Planning and Implementation of Observation

All scientific observations need to be planned and executed systematically. While planning for observations the following important aspects have to be considered:

1. The individual who develops observational study must have a sound background of theory and knowledge in the area of his study. As pointed by Walter R. Borg, "Without this theoretical foundation and an extensive background of knowledge, the observational study often yield inconclusive information that is difficult to express in quantitative terms."
2. Carefully select and define precisely and preciously the activities to be observed. This will save time and help the observer to concentrate on relevant facts only. In defining the activities, the purpose is to include those activities truly representative of the general category under study. The validity of results to a large extent depends on how well the investigator selects his activities and defines them.
3. The next important aspect to be considered is formulation of testable hypotheses. It is essential to develop specific hypotheses relating to the observable behaviour to the variable being studied. The hypotheses may be refined in course of the research.

4. Decide the size of units to be observed. Observation being a time consuming and expensive technique, one cannot observe and record all the behaviour that takes place in a given situation, but only a fragment of the population. Therefore, steps should be taken to obtain representative sample of the behaviour to be observed. As observed by *Dr. M.H. Gopal,* "this sample may relate to the person to be observed each at a particular time or of certain key aspects of behaviour to be observed all the time or of observation of the time or of observation of the whole group during a particular period of time." In order to obtain reliable data, it is necessary to know something of the universe and must be careful in choosing the sample to be observed. It is always risky to use sampling procedure unless one has an adequate theory to guide the selection of the sample.
5. Decide the type of observation technique to be used. The observation may be carried on in natural surroundings on non-controlled basis or on a laboratory type experimental basis. The choice of observational technique, of course, depends on the nature and purpose of his study. In all cases, proper arrangements must be made for objective observation.
6. Determine the period to be observed which involves the length of each period, number of periods and interval between periods. The process of observation may be of short duration or may be for a long period. Generally, the length of period of observation is related to the type of activity under study. Sometimes period of a minute or two are suitable for some situations where a time period of an hour or even more may prove as more useful for other activities or aspects of behaviour.
7. Select appropriate aids and mechanical devices to be employed to obtain adequate data and to achieve greater objectivity. There are a number of devices which are used as aids in field observation such as detailed field notes, schedules and questionnaires,

maps, photographs, socio-metric scales, motion pictures, tape recorders, films etc.

8. Decide the number of observers needed. The observation may be done by the researcher himself or by a team of observers depends on the nature of the study. As the reliability of observation depends on the quality of the observer, he should possess a number of qualities. These personal qualities are the most important. He should be physically fit, intellectually sharp and alert. He must have genuine interest and aptitude for research. He should be quite adjustable, courteous and also be very cautious in asking questions pertaining to sentiments or secret matters. He should deal very cautiously with illiterates as his questions may react adversely with his understanding.

9. Arrange for expert training to the observers. Efficiency and objectivity can be attained through training of observers. If observers are not properly trained his observation may lead to inaccuracy. Such inaccuracy is of two kinds: *(i)* failure to see, resulting in non-observation of the important issues; and *(ii)* seeing things wrongly i.e., mal observation. Both these errors are due to the shortcomings in the observer himself, who is in a sense, a measuring instrument." In observation it is not so much the physical side of seeing that is most important, but the psychological side which means skilled seeing. The training process requires that the observers: *(i)* be familiar with the theoretical framework of the purposes of the investigation; *(ii)* have experiences in which they become sensitive to the dimensions under considerations, *(iii)* have extensive training, experience with the proposed observation schedule, including a trial run, preferably with a group like that which they will be observing, *(iv)* have training in the use of mechanical aids, *(v)* have discussion on problems in selecting proper categories, sampling and keeping up with the events; *(vi)* have a discussion

on the observation form describing each item sufficiently to develop a thorough understanding of what is to be observed and how it is to be recorded. During the training period, one may come across observers who cannot develop to interpret the behaviour they observe consistently. In such cases, it is advisable to replace such persons with other observers. Thus, a proper and well designed training programme will overcome most of the personal deficiencies in the observer.

10. Arrange for preliminary observation. A preliminary observation may be conducted to perfect the observation form. It also helps in the efficient conduct of the main study and provides guidance to overcome several practical problems.

11. Arrange for proper recording of data. Once entered into the field and decided to have the type of relationship with the subject, the observer should focus on the recording of the observation. In recording the observation two questions require consideration: What should the observer make notes? How should the notes be kept? As observers cannot remember all the events, some method of recording observations is necessary. Similarly, he cannot write detailed notes while he is observing since it would disturb the naturalness of the situation and result in diversion of attention. Therefore, he has to make mental notes of what is observed. Afterwards he can prepare the detailed field notes. Fields notes are the running descriptions of participants, events, settings and behaviours. The writing of field notes should be done as soon as possible to minimize personal biases and distortion through memory. The notes may be in narrative form.

12. After data have been collected, the researcher has to pay full attention to their analysis and interpretation. By means of organizing, analyzing and interpreting the data their salient features, inter-relationship and cause and relationship are brought

out. Information collected through observation should be interpreted scientifically.

Advantages of Observation

Observation has some distinct advantages which are listed below:

1. Observation is one of the simplest and non-technical methods. Observational studies can be conducted by person through proper training.
2. It is one of the common methods used in all sciences and therefore it is systematized.
3. It is one of the main sources of formulating hypotheses.
4. Observation helps to study the subject in-depth.
5. It helps in the free flow of information as the situation is not disturbed.
6. It is possible to record behaviour as it occurs.
7. It is a very useful technique of studying various activities and characteristics of infants and children.
8. The researcher is able to record natural behaviours of the group.
9. The researcher can collect a wide range of information.
10. The data collected through observation is more reliable and valid than otherwise.
11. It is a useful method of doing research in delicate areas.
12. This method involves less expense.

Limitations

Though observation is a widely used technique, it has its own limitations. They are discussed below:

1. All occurrences may not be open to observation. For instance, the personal activities are not open to actual observation by an outsider.

2. Personal bias of the observer at times distorts the observation.
3. Observation of phenomena has to be made where it actually takes place. Most of the occurrences are quite uncertain in nature. Their place and time cannot be predetermined. Therefore, systematic and preplanned observation is very difficult.
4. Sometimes, natural factors, such as weather conditions, side attractions and the like may affect the observational task.
5. There are difficulties in sampling. Sometimes, it is not possible to ensure that participants represent a cross-section of the population.
6. It may be impossible for the researcher to collect all the necessary information if the events spread over a period of years or the events occur simultaneously in different geographic locations.

20

Scaling Techniques

In recent days greater emphasis is laid on the measuring instruments in social sciences research. Scaling is a technique used for measurement of some aspects of human behaviour by means of a precise scale. In its simplest form of measurement consists of substituting symbol or name of a real object. According to Barnard S. Phillip, "Scaling is a procedure for assignment of numbers (or their symbols) to a property or object in order to impart some of the characteristics of numbers to the property in question."

Scaling techniques are useful in measuring the social behaviour and personality of individuals. It is also used to measure certain aspects of cultural and social environment. Scaling serves the following specific purposes in social sciences research:

1. Scales help to reduce the complexity of data and present a single score that represents several variables.
2. It helps to test hypotheses by means of quantifying different dimensions of a single underlying concept.
3. It aims at reducing the error in measurement and increasing the reliability of analysis.

The scales may be broadly classified into following types:

1. Nominal
2. Ordinal
3. Rating and
4. Ratio

1. Nominal Scale

When the measurement is made with help of an arbitrary number or symbol it is called Nominal scale. It is generally used to distinguish one property or objectives from other properties. It helps to determine whether the object belongs to the same class or not. For example, we may classify the individuals as athletes, politicians,.students, etc. The nominal scale has the following characteristics:

- Nominal scales are used to classify the objects,
- The classifications do not overlap,
- Nominal scales are discrete, and
- Nominal scales result in measurement process.

Although nominal scales may look like a simple technique, the measurement becomes more complex when a given property or variable becomes complex. For example a nominal scale for the classification of societies into 'scared' and 'secular' ones cannot be easily evolved. Besides, the normal scale implies the division of objects categorically. There may be border-line cases which may be difficult to judge as to which category they belong. There is also an element of arbitrariness in nominal scale. The scale is not sensitive to various gradations within a given category.

2. Ordinal Scale

The ordinal scale is used when there is some kind of relationship between two or more classes of objects. It incorporates order relationship manifested by numbers, the number indicating rank in this context. "The rater places the person or object being rated at some point along a continuum or in one of an ordered series of categories and a numerical value attached to the point of category". In other words, the numbers are simply rank ordered. For example, if A,B, and C receive leadership scores of 15, 20, and 5 respectively, as an ordinal scale one may say that A is superior to B and B is superior to C.

However, the social science researcher comes across several social phenomena which cannot be simply rank ordered, as the property of a phenomenon may not be unitary in character. Another limitation of the ordinal scale is that it permits only a limited statistical application. While constructing the ordinal scale, the researcher is presented with two tasks.

1. To order the objects with respect to a given property through the assignment of ranks, and
2. To determine whether the actual phenomena posses the order characteristics of number.

3. *Rating Scale/Interval Scale*

A rating scale ascertains in the degree, intensity or frequency of a variable. It not only places entities in a clearly defined order, but also utilizes some means of attaining equidistant intervals of measurement. This scale permits one to say that the distance between A and B equals the distance of B and C but it does not permit to say that A with the score of 15 is thrice as good as C and B with the score of 10 is twice as good as C.

To construct such a scale an investigator identifies the factors to be measured, places units or categories on a scale to differentiate varying degrees of that factor and describes these units in some manner. No established rule governs the number of units that should be placed on a scale. The rating scale is amenable for statistical calculations like Mean, Standard Deviation, and Product Moment Correlation etc. In this type of scale the zero point is arbitrary and just a matter of convenience. Different types of Rating/Interval scale are used to judge the persons or objects. The more common types among them are explained below.

A. Graphic Rating Scale

This is perhaps the most widely used scale. In this method the researcher indicates his rating by simply placing a check at the appropriate point on a line that consists of brief statements indicating one extreme of the phenomenon to the other extreme. Scale points may also be indicated along the line. The scale serves as a guide in locating the rating rather than to provide distinct categories. This type of scale is relatively easy to use. For example, the following graphic rating scale may be used to enable the student to rate the instructor.

Graphic Rating Scale

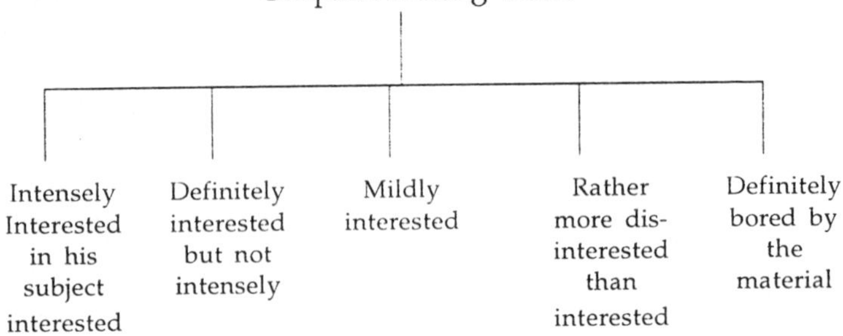

B. Itemized Rating Scale

This type of scale consists of a number of statements that are ordered in respect of their scale positions. The rater selects one or two of the categories. Though the number of categories or scale positions varies depending on the research problem, normally five or seven categories are used. The verbal statements used to identify the scale positions may vary from brief statements indicating only degree of attributes to more elaborate descriptions and illustrations. The more clearly defined the categories are, the more reliable the ratings are likely to be.

C. Comparative Rating Scale

Comparative Rating Scale is used for relative judgment. The position of individual in the rating scale is judged with reference to the position of other individuals or groups with which the individual may be compared. For example, a questionnaire used in evaluating an employee may contain a question regarding the efficiency of the employee compared with other employees. Is the employee more efficient than 10 percent of them? 20 percent of them or 30 percent of them? Here, the rater has to make comparative judgment.

This kind of scale is difficult to construct and the rater must also have a clear conception of not only individuals but also the whole group. Another kind of comparative rating scale is Rank Order Scale, in which the judge is required to rank the individual specifically in relation to one another. The rater has to indicate rank of individual from the highest to the lowest in regard to the characteristic being measured. This kind of rating is possible only when the investigator is concerned with a limited group of people.

4. *Ratio Scale*

It is the highest type of scale. It possesses all the characteristics of an interval scale. In addition to that, it is characterized by an absolute zero, which offers a consistent starting point for measurement. With such a scale, one can speak of relative amounts as well as difference in the amount and property or characteristic. It also determines the equality of ratios. However, the ratio-scales have not been well developed in social sciences. In the opinion of Jahoda, et al., "For most of the subject matter of social sciences, we are far from having devised procedures that satisfy the requirements of a ratio scale."

5. *Attitude Scale*

Fundamentally scale in methodology is same to all fields. Differences do exist in content, emphasis and purpose for which scales are used. In the social sciences like sociology, psychology and in many other interdisciplinary researches, the most frequently used scaling technique is Attitude Scale. Therefore, it is of very great significance to social scientists. Different types of attitude scales are in vogue. They differ from each other in method of construction, method of response and basis of interpreting the scale. The important types of attitude scales are discussed in this section.

A. Differential Scale

This technique of Equal Appearing Interval method was evolved by L.L. Thurston which has become the widely applied scale. In this scale the items from a gradation of such a nature that the individual is likely to agree with one or two statements which correspond to his position in the dimension being measured. He is likely to disagree with statements on either side of the position he has selected. Thurston type of scale consists of a series of statements, usually about twenty. The position of each statement on a scale of favourable/unfavourable attitude towards the object has been determined by the judges' classification. In selecting the items for the scale and assigning values to them, following procedure is adopted.

1. The researcher gathers several hundred statements conceived to be related to attitude being investigated.
2. A large number of judges—usually from fifty to three hundred—working independently, classify these statements into eleven groups. In the first pile, each judge places the statements considered most favourable to the object in the second, those considered next most favourable, and the eleventh pile, most unfavourable. The sixth or 'neutral' position is defined as the point at which there is neither favourableness nor unfavourableness.
3. The scale value of the statement is computed as the median position (or pile) to which it is assigned by the group of judges. Statements that have too broad a scatter are discarded as ambiguous or irrelevant.
4. A final selection is made taking such items that are spread out evenly along the scale from one extreme position to the other.

The scale value are not shown on the questionnaire. Items are arranged in random order rather than in the order of their scale value. The individual's position in the scale is judged by the mean for the scale value.

B. Summated Scale

Summated scale, like differential scale, consists of a set of statements to which the subject is asked to react. The number of statements affecting a phenomenon is listed and values given to each. Respondents are asked to indicate their agreement or disagreement with each item. Each response is given a numerical score indicating its favourableness. For example, to understand one's attitude towards cooperative, the attitude scale may consist of the following statements:

	Strongly Agree	*Agree*	*Undecided*	*Disagree*	*Strongly disagree*
1. Co-operatives are rendering useful service to public	5	4	3	2	1
2. Co-operatives have lot of corruption	1	2	3	4	5

The score given to individual items are summed up. The most frequently used summated scale is the Likert type of scale. Rensis Likert has developed an elaborate technique of constructing a summated scale, as outlined below:

1. The score includes five categories of responses; strongly agree, agree, undecided, disagree and strongly disagree.
2. Statements are classified into those which are favourable and those which are unfavourable.
3. For favourable statements weight given to strongly agree, agree, undecided, disagree, strongly disagree are 5,4,3,2,1, respectively; and for unfavourable statements, the weights given are 1,2,3,4, and 5 respectively. Thus, agreement with favourable statements and disagreement with unfavourable statements are treated as equals.

4. A large number of statements are administered to a group of respondents who are representative of those for whom the questionnaire is being constructed.
5. The responses are analyzed to determine which items discriminate between the high scoring individuals and low scoring individuals. Thus, for example items to which high scorers and low scorers respond similarly are eliminated. This is known as item analysis procedure.

C. Cumulative Scale

Cumulative Scales, like differential and summated scales are made up a series of items with which the respondents indicate agreement or disagreement. In cumulative scale, items are arranged in such a way that they are related to one another. They are arranged logically that an individual who replies favourably to item 2 also replies favourably to item 1; and one who replies favourably to item 1 and 2. An individual who has given favourable response to more number of items in the scale will be higher total score. The individual's score is computed by counting the number of items one answers favourably. The items are arranged in the order of favourableness. The Social Distance Scale developed by Bogardus was a cumulative type of attitude scale.

Guttman and his colleagues developed a scale analysis of "Scalogram", which is referred to by Guttman as the 'Cornell' technique. The steps involved in 'Scalogram' analysis is given below:

1. The area of content is first defined with reference to the problem on hand.
2. Ten or twelve statements are selected which are assumed to be representative of the selected area.
3. The statements are usually arranged in the form of a three or five point scale, so that subjects can indicate their intensity of their attitude for each item.

4. Ten or twelve items are submitted to a sample of 100 or more respondents' who will check the items. The step is designed to determine the scalability of the item.
5. After the total score is obtained for each person by adding up the weights of the categories checked, the questionnaires are arranged in the rank order from high to low according to the total score.
6. A table or 'Scalogram' is prepared from the data of the questionnaires, by recording separately the responses of each person to each category, by providing a column for each person and a row for each category.
7. The reproducibility of each item is determined on the basis that no person with a lower total score ranks higher in any item than any person with a higher total score. By this method the error in reproducibility is minimized.

Principles of Scale Construction

A researcher is performing one of the most important tasks when selecting and constructing a scale with a view to evaluating it. The evaluation is done on the following criteria.

1. Validity

A test is valid when it measures what it purports to measure. This is the most significant criterion in the use of scale. A scale is valid when the following two conditions are met:

1. The attribute being measured where relatively 'objective' so that their meaning would be uniformly understood by the raters using the scale.
2. The ratings themselves were obtained under optimal conditions, including the carefully constructed scales, trained judges and specified common frames of references.

Validity of test also varies with the circumstances. A

test may be highly valid for use in the situation but invalid if used in another situation. Therefore, validity must be appraised with reference to specific situation.

2. *Reliability*

"A test or scale is reliable if it consistently yields the same result when repeated measurements are taken of the same subject under the same conditions." Reliability suggests consistency and accuracy from one time to another. The errors of measurement should be reduced to the minimum and the measuring instrument should possess a degree of precision. Reliability can be increased by the following measures:

- Careful training of the rater
- Attention given in the construction of scale
- Clear specification of the reference group
- Inclusion of concrete illustration of the question response, types of behaviour and proper communication.

3. *Objectivity*

An objective test or scale is one that produces the same score regardless of who makes it. The scoring should be independent of personal judgment of the selector. In order to improve the objective specific directions or scoring keys should be furnished to the scorer, that allows no room for subjective judgment.

4. *Simplicity*

Simplicity enables their use to many. Ease of administration, scoring and interpretation is an important factor in selecting a test, particularly when expert personnel and adequate budget are not available.

5. *Suitability*

When selecting a scale one must determine whether the instrument is suitable for the purpose. The researcher has to examine whether he can obtain the data needed or suited to the type of subjects studied. A prudent researcher must carefully examine the appropriateness of the testing instruments. Even a best instrument may fail to yield reliable data, if it is improperly administered, under inappropriate conditions and inaccurately interpreted.

6. *Economy*

Tests should save time involved. The expense in administration is often a significant factor, particularly if the testing programme is operated on a limited budget.

21

Use of Library in Research

Man's knowledge lies silently in his libraries. The knowledge of all time is to be found in these store houses of black marks on white paper. A library has been recognized as in important aid in self education. The concepts of library and library services have acquired new dimensions in recent years. With the advancement of education and research in different fields in post independence period, the National and State Governments had been taking various steps to improve the library system in the country. The function of library is to provide information and authentic reference on various subjects to users. As Rabindranath Tagore said at All India Library Conference in 1928, "Most libraries are possessed with the passion for accumulation. The facilities offered for their (books) use that should have been its (a library's) glory, and not deemed necessary for its pride." Thus, the primary purpose of a library is not only to lend books, journals and other materials but also to encourage the formation of a life long habit of reading library resources by making necessary facilities to the users.

All types of researches involve the use of books, reports, journals, magazines, news papers and other documentary materials in libraries. A research student has to tap various sources of data which may vary with this interest and the type of his study. Sources of data may be grouped differently: *(i)* available material and original data; *(ii)* primary and secondary data; and *(iii)* bibliographical and field data. But the most commonly used classification is primary, secondary and tertiary sources. Dr. P.V. Young has defined primary sources, as those data gathered at first hand, the responsibility of their compilation and promulgation remaining, under the same authority that originally gathered them. According to Walter R. Borg primary sources is direct description of occurrence by an individual who actually observed or witnessed the occurrence. Secondary data are those compiled from original sources and of which the promulgating authority is different from that which controlled the collection of data at first hand. In other words, secondary materials include any publications written by an author who was not a direct observer or participant in the events described. For example, for statistical and factual data on baking problems, bank records are primary sources, the Reserve Bank of India's statistics secondary source and books, written on banking are tertiary sources.

Writers like Dr. P.V. Young has classified the sources of data into field and documentary sources, "Field sources include living person who have a fund of knowledge about or have been in intimate contact with social conditions and changes over a considerable period of time." Observation interview, questionnaire and other devices are used to gather adequate information from the field. Documentary sources include published and unpublished documents, reports, statistics, letters and diaries.

A researcher should make the maximum use of the library sources as there is a wealth of information and materials in the academic libraries. The researcher is warned not to hurry into the field without first consulting the necessary books, journals, past and present investigations of relevance, official reports and statistics, records of institutions etc. Consulting available library material will be useful to a researcher in several ways:

1. Library sources provide the necessary background

knowledge of the problem to be investigated and develop the insight of the investigator.

2. It helps the researcher to review the literature to find out the research gap which is the basis of most of the research projects in social sciences;
3. It also provides orientation to the problem and eliminates the possibility of unnecessary duplication of effort.
4. The use of documentary source facilitates in the formulation of research hypotheses;
5. Library literature provides an opportunity of understanding the method, techniques measures and approaches employed by other research workers and thus lead to significant improvement of his design;
6. Secondary sources of data gathered from library serve as base for analysis and comparative study;
7. The available documents may also be used to supplement or to check information gathered by the researcher in his investigations;
8. Where research consists more in interpretation than in the discovery of new facts, secondary sources would be more than adequate;
9. Authors of research articles may cite specific research topics for further research, which would be of great use to young researchers;
10. The knowledge secured from library reading will also help a researcher to understand the writing style and interpretation of findings.

I. The Essentials

The researcher must be capable of: *(i)* locating the necessary sources, *(ii)* deciding what is to be extracted from each source, and *(iii)* taking relevant notes needed.

All libraries have a system of subject classification, a card catalogue and certain bibliographic and reference materials. A researcher must have knowledge of the card catalogue, the indexes and the reference shelves to locate easily the needed secondary sources.

Card catalogue is an index which lists all the publications in the library collection by author, by subject, and by title. This is perhaps the first source to find materials in a library. It is arranged like a dictionary with the cards filed alphabetically according to the first word on the card. The name of the author, the subject heading or the title of the publication may be the first word. The researcher may seek the help of the librarian to use card catalogue.

The card catalogue may not always index all the materials that are available in the library. Further, the card catalogue lists every periodical available in bound volumes but it does not analyze the contents. There are periodicals articles, pamphlets, magazines and government documents which form important segments of published materials may be organized and maintained separately in certain libraries. Therefore, a researcher must use the indexes kept in the reference shelves as guide for finding out materials. Indexes may be general or specialized. Thus, indexes supplement the card catalogue.

There are also encyclopedias, special dictionaries, year books, directories, abstracts etc. in a library. These reference materials may not be indexed in the card catalogue or in indexes because of their general character. As these serve a useful purpose, a researcher must have knowledge of the above sources which are kept in the reference shelves. Some of the important such sources are listed and described briefly in the following section.

1. Bibliographies

Bibliographic tool is commonly used in finding materials in libraries. A bibliography covers information regarding books, articles etc. published in a specific period in a particular subject. Each book or article is listed by author, title, place of publication. The important bibliographies are listed below:

2. *Internal Bibliography of Social Sciences*

It is published by UNESCO since 1952. It is published annually in four parts—Economics, Political Science, Sociology and Anthropology. The important publications in four subjects are included in this bibliography.

3. *Indian National Bibliography*

This is an authoritative record of current publications in the 15 major languages of India, received by the National Library, Calcutta.

4. *Asia Social Science Bibliography*

This is the publication of the Institute of the Economic Growth, New Delhi. It covers subjects like Economics, Sociology, Anthropology, Political Science, Education and Communication and other social data.

5. *Bibliography of Research Studies in Education*

This is published by US Office of Education since 1941. This is organized by subject areas.

6. *Bibliography of Doctoral Thesis in Arts and Science*

This is a valuable guide published by the Inter University Board of India. Theses accepted by the Indian Universities are listed under University, with subject sub-headings.

7. *ICA Research Register*

The research register is an ICA project within the frame work of the cooperative development decade. It has been published by the Cooperative Research Institute, Hungary in collaboration with the ICA. Information about the recently published books, articles and research works are reported author-wise and subject-wise. It is a very good reference to those who do research in the areas of cooperation.

II. Indexes

As started earlier, indexes serve as useful tool to locate

information in recent journals, magazines etc. They also summarize the contents of the articles and cite the reference cited by author in a particular article while it was written. Generally, the indexed items include the name of the author title of the article, name of the journal, its volume number, periodicity, month and year of publication and pagination of a particular article. A social science researcher can make use of the following indexes:

1. Social Sciences Index

This is published in two parts: *(1) Social Science Index* and *(2) Humanities Index*. It is published by H.W. Wilson and Co., New York.

2. Social Science Citation Index

It is published by the Institute of Scientific Information, 325 Chestnut Street, Philadelphia, U.S.A. It is a multi-dimensional index to social science. This international publication indexes about 70,000 articles and important editorial from over 1,000 of the world's standard social sciences journals, belong to 26 disciplines.

3. Cord Index

It is published by the National Institute of Rural Development, Hyderabad. It is a systematic listing of the rural development literature published in over six hundred journals and thirteen news papers received in the card library. Particular requirements of the research scholars in socio-economic development are kept in mind while indexing the articles. This index includes subject like agriculture and allied areas, education and training, energy, health and nutrition, industry, manpower, political science and rural and tribal development.

4. A Manual of Sources of Data on the Tamilnadu Economy

It is one of the publications of the Madras Institute of Development Studies, Madras. This index aims to fill the information gap relating to the Tamilnadu Economy. It is the work of its kind listing in a systematic manner data sources on the Tamilnadu Economy that researchers can have access to. The information contained in index shows that an impressive body of official and semi-official data pertaining to Tamilnadu economy is available to researchers.

5. *Index India*

The Rajasthan University has been publishing this index since 1967. It is a quarterly publication indexes book reviews, theses, articles published in Indian and foreign journals and Indian news papers.

III. Dictionaries

There are dictionaries that serve special purpose and interest. They define basic concepts used in different social science subjects. They include the following:

1. *A Dictionary of the Social Sciences*

Edited by Julius Gould William L. Kolb and compiled under the auspices of the United Nations Educational Scientific and Cultural Organization. It is designed to describe and define one thousand basic concepts used in the Social Sciences.

2. *Dictionary of Modern Economics*

By Douglas Greenwald Associates (1973) published by McGraw Hill Book Company, New York. It provides a simple definition of modern economic terms.

3. *Dictionary of Banking*

By Rev. Jones. It is a concise encyclopedia of Banking Law and Practice. It provides in one volume the information about any subject connected with the business of baking.

4. *A Modern Dictionary of Sociology*

By George A. Theodorson and Achillies G. Theodorson. It defines modern sociological terms used in popular books, magazines news papers, on the radio and on television. As many concepts as possible as included.

5. *Dictionary of Psychology*

Edited by Howard C. Warran, George Allen and Unwin Ltd., London; 1934. This book is designed to explain the meaning and technical terms which the reader will meet in psychological literature or which the scholar in the field of psychology wishes to use in his writings.

6. *Dictionary of Philosophy*

Edited by Dagobert D. Runes, Little Field Adam and Co, New Jersey; 1964. This aims at providing researchers interested in philosophy with clear, concise and correct definitions and descriptions of the philosophic terms throughout the range of philosophic though.

7. *The New Dictionary of Thoughts*

By Tryon Edwards, Standard Book Co., New York: 1953. It was first published in 1877. It is a very useful condensed dictionary which describes the striking thoughts of the world's best thinkers on important and interesting subjects arranged in alphabetical order of topic for ready reference.

8. *Dictionary of Education*

Edited by Carter V. Goode and published by Mcgraw Hill Book Co. in 1959. It is concerned with technical and professional terms and concepts in the entire area of education.

IV. Encyclopedias

Encyclopedias are huge or multi-volume work containing articles of both biographical and general character. They are the standard works done by experts in the various fields of social science. The articles in the encyclopedias are arranged alphabetically. An article in an encyclopedia can be useful for quick orientation to a subject and for specific items of information.

1. *Encyclopedia Britannica*

By William Beton, Chicago. A new survey of universal

knowledge alphabetically and systematically arranged. Today the Britanica consisted of 23 volumes. It is a modern informational instrument in a changing and complex world. It is the work of 9000 authorities from most of the countries of the world. This is a very good reference containing information on every essential subject.

2. *Encyclopedia of Social Science*

It is published in 15 volumes. It combines the characteristics of both a dictionary and hand book. It is arranged so flexible as to contain not only short articles but also long articles. A carefully worked out system of cross references are given to meet the special interest of scholars. It also includes biographies of deceased persons whose work has been significant in social sciences. A scholar can find factual and methodical information of value and also inter-relationship between the social sciences.

3. *Encyclopedia of Parliament*

By Norman Wilding and Philip Landy, Cassell and Co, London: 1958. This attempts to present wide range of parliamentary information in the form of an encyclopedia. It is a valuable work of reference to researchers in political science and public information.

V. Year-Books and Directories

The researchers can find current information and latest data on different subjects in the yearbook and directories. Some of the important yearbooks and directories are listed below:

1. *Yearbook of International Organization*

It is the publication of the Union of International Associations, Brussels. It was published since 1948. Information about international organizations are included in the book.

2. *Yearbook of Agricultural Cooperation*

This yearbook had been published by the Plunkett

Foundation for Cooperative Studies since 1927. The purpose is to provide a continuous review of agricultural cooperative development throughout the world, from a wide range of view points by publishing articles on countries at regular intervals and on particular aspect of cooperation which are innovative or on topical interest. It is a useful source for researchers in cooperation.

3. *Cooperative Yearbook*

It is a compact book published by the Tamilnadu Cooperative Union, which gives all that we want to know about cooperatives in Tamilnadu. The progress of the cooperative movement in general and the constitution and working of individual cooperatives are presented in this work.

4. *Indian Poultry Industry Yearbook*

It is a comprehensive single volume of reference data on various aspect of poultry industry in India. It was first published by Shakuntala P. Guptha on behalf of the Government of India in 1973.

5. *India—A Reference Annual*

It is published by the Research and Reference Division, Ministry of Information and Broadcasting, Government of India. It is an established and popular books of reference, seek to provide authentic information on the diverse aspects of our life, administration and economy. The data furnished in this volume include subject like agriculture, education, industry community, development, communication, irrigation and power, housing, commerce, planning, health, social welfare, scientific research, defense etc.

6. *Tamilnadu—An Economic Appraisal*

This is the publication of Finance Department, Government of Tamilnadu, it provides data regarding diverse of Tamilnadu Economy.

7. *Asian Business Directory*

It is an exhaustive in-depth reference manual for business, trade and industry in Asia and Pacific published by Kothari and Sons for the Asian Chambers of Commerce and Industry. It gives not only facts and figures, about each country but also laws affecting investment, foreign trade and the like.

8. *Directory and Year Book (1980-81)*

Edited by Girilal Jain and published by the Times of India Press, Mumbai. It contains a wide range of information about the country, natural resources, agro-based industries, education and science, welfare programmes demography, trade and industry, finance, communicating, administrative and diplomatic matters, elections and legislatures.

9. *Directory of Scientific Research in Indian Universities*

It was published by the Council of Scientific and Industrial Research, New Delhi since 1974. The directory covers current research projects in the field of agriculture, transport, industry and management carried out in the universities and other educational institutions in India.

10. *Directory of Indian Women Today (1976)*

Edited by Ajeet Cour and published by India International Publications. The material in this directory gives us a microscopic estimate of the women power in India; it is very useful and purposeful publication for researchers.

11. *Directory of Educational Research Institutions in the Asian Region*

It was published by UNESCO Regional Office for Education in Asia, Bangkok since 1967. It gives information about 107 institutions engaged in the research in the field of education including government agencies, universities and autonomous institutions in 18 countries.

VI. Abstracts

An abstract is another type of reference guide useful to a researcher. It is a systematized list of reference source. It also gives a brief summary of the contents of articles or research studies listed.

1. World Agricultural Economics and Rural Sociology Abstracts

It is published by North Holland Publishing Company, Amsterdam. It is a quarterly international abstract which covers subjects like agriculture, farm labour, marketing, agricultural economics and rural sociology.

2. ICSSR Research Abstracts

It is a quarterly and commenced publication in October 1971. The major findings of the research projects financed by the Council are published in this journal.

3. ICSSR Abstracts

There are such journals for the subject's sociology and social anthropology, economics, geography, political science. In these half-yearly journals, abstracts of select articles and reviews of selected books are published.

4. Indian Dissertation Abstract

It is a quarterly published under the joint auspices of the ICSSR and the Association of Indian Universities. This publishes synopsis of Ph.D. thesis in social sciences submitted to Indian Universities.

5. Student Research Abstracts in Social Work

It was published by the Association of Schools of Social Work in India since 1968. This is an abstract of research works. The topics studied by the students include the major aspects of family and child welfare, medical and psychiatric social work, labour welfare, industrial relations and personnel management, urban, rural and tribal community organizations, social defense, social welfare administration etc. This abstract will serve as a useful guide to future researcher. The analysis of these abstracts would help identifying gaps in information and at the same time discourage scholars from undertaking the projects already done.

6. *Indian Behavioural Science Abstracts*

This contains abstracts of behavioural science literature produced in India and abroad. It is published by Behavioural Science Centre, Delhi. It is a quarterly publication covers disciplines like psychology, sociology, social anthropology, education, management, political science, extension education, human geography, economics, etc.

7. *CORD Abstracts*

It is a monthly bulletin of abstracts of selected development literature published by the National Institute of Rural Development, Hyderabad. It provides information abstracts for the reports, articles based on the empirical studies relating to rural India. Abstracts aim to bring out the salient features of these studies, keeping in view of the needs of researchers. It is arranged alphabetically subject-wise.

VII. Statistical Sources

There are a large number of statistical statements relating to socio-economic problems which are published by Governments, cooperatives and private agencies. These statements are very useful for social science researchers.

1. *Demographic Yearbook*

It is being published since 1948 by the United Nations Department of Economic and Social Affairs, New York. It is one of the coordinated and inter-related set of periodic publications issued by the United Nations and the specialized agencies, designed to supply basic statistical data for social scientists and scholars. Official demographic statistics from almost 250 geographic entities of the world are included in the issue.

2. *United Nations Statistical Yearbook*

The U.N. Department of Economic and Social Affairs, New York, publishes the yearbook annually. This contains country-wise statistics on population, national income, agriculture, energy, external trade, transport and industrial production.

3. *Census of India*

This volume is being published once in ten years by the Government of India in different series. This is the largest single source of data. Data presented in this volume relate to diverse aspects of population in the country.

4. *Statistical Abstracts of India*

This is published by the Central Statistical Organization, Department of Statistics, Ministry of Planning, Government of India. This incorporates the latest available date under important heads of economic and social development. It gives national aggregates for 1950-51, 1955-56, 1960-61, 1965-66, 1970-71 and for the subsequent year up to 1977-78. This serves as an important source material for authentic data on different sectors of the Indian economy.

5. *Statistical Statements—Khadi and Village Industries Commission*

It is a useful statistical supplement that aims at projecting a detailed picture of the state-wise, and industry-wise performance in selected indicators of progress such as extension of finance, production, sales, employment and earnings, besides a broad summary of achievements.

6. *Indian Labour Statistics*

It is published annually by the Labour Bureau, Ministry of Labour, Government of India. It contains statistics relating to labour in India Covering population census, economic data, employment in factories, mines, railways, plantations, employment exchanges, training centers, wages and earnings in different sectors, levels of living, industrial disputes, trade unions and such other matters relating to labour in India.

7. Statistical Tables Relating to Banks in India

It is one of the annual publications of the RBI. This presents an alphabetical list of bank offices. Offices of Indian banks abroad and such other information relevant to the geographic aspects of the bank's operation.

8. Indian Agriculture in Brief

This is annually published by the Union Ministry of Agriculture and Irrigation. It contains data relating to Indian Agriculture.

9. Hand-Book on Social Welfare Statistics

It is a publication made by the Department of Social Welfare, Ministry of Education and Social Welfare, Government of India. It was brought out first in 1974. It provides valuable statistical information about the social welfare programmes implemented in India. The statistics that are included in this handbook covers areas like demography, health and family planning, education, employment, housing, backward classes, rehabilitation, levels of living, leisure and recreation, international comparisons, child welfare, women welfare, welfare of physically handicapped, social defense, social work education, training and research, social security etc.

10. Statistical Statements Relating to Cooperatives

This is published annually by the NABARD in two Parts; Part-1 contains data regarding the working of agricultural cooperatives in the country. Part-2 deals with non-agricultural cooperatives. District-wise information are well presented in these statements.

Collection and Organization of Materials

1. Background Reading

Once the researcher has decided to take a workable

project he should go through as many literatures as possible to gather useful information. This is to be done with the main object of knowing whether the reference has any direct or indirect bearing on the subject under study. For this purpose the researcher can go through the table of contents of the sources. It is on the basis of this that references found useful are to be listed in a bibliography.

2. *Development of a Bibliography*

The next important step is compiling a bibliography. Such a bibliography should be complete, accurate in every detail and consistent in form i.e., following a uniform classification.

A Card index would facilitate easy reference, alterations, and additions and save duplication. The sources may be classified with general and specialized data and books, periodicals, news papers and reports—official and non-officials. Each reference should appear on a separate card or sheet with author's name, title of reference, publisher's name, date of publication, page number etc.

3. *Preliminary Outline*

The next step is to prepare a rough outline for what is to be extracted from each source. This depends upon the problem selected, the type of investigation, the researcher's experience and the availability of material.

4. *Evaluation of Material*

Before deciding to include any information, the researcher should evaluate the materials carefully. The following points are to be kept in mind while evaluating the material:

1. Accuracy and dependability
2. Up-to-datedness
3. Suitability for specific requirements
4. Authority
5. Scope

6. Treatment and style
7. Arrangement
8. Illustrations, tables and diagrams
9. Author
10. Publisher.

Notes-Taking

After locating the information that the researcher wants, the next problem is to record it for further use. Notes-taking is not an easy job. It requires much time and patience "Method, adequacy and accuracy are the three important ingredients of notes. Good notes should help analysis by isolating facts and synthesis by combining them. The more careful the researcher is in notes-taking the greater will be the benefit from his effort." The notes may be classified into four categories: *(i)* quotations *(ii)* paraphrases, *(iii)* summary, and *(iv)* evaluation.

The researcher may keep in mind the following points while taking notes:

1. Decide what material is to be extracted and recorded.
2. Select the most significant material.
3. Make each note on a separate card. Use always 4 X 6 uniform cards. Different colour cards may be used for different categories of notes.
4. Include only one topic on a card.
5. Make the entries complete and accurate.
6. Place the subject heading on the top of the card.
7. Give a complete and accurate bibliographic citation at the bottom of the card.
8. Distinguish between a direct quotation, a summary and an evaluative statement.
9. Record correctly all the information that are needed.
10. Keep the notes orderly filed.

SECTION – V

RESEARCH DESIGN AND REPORT WRITING

22

Preparation of Research Design

Meaning

A research design is a logical and systematic plan prepared for directing a research study. It specifies the objectives of the study, the methodology and techniques to be adopted for achieving the objectives. It "constitutes the blue print for the collection, measurement and analysis of data." It is "the plan, structure and strategy of investigation conceived so as to obtain answer to research questions.... The plan is the overall scheme or programme of research." "A research design is the programme that guides the investigator in the process of collecting, analyzing and interpreting observations." "It provides a systematic plan of procedure for the researcher to follow."

Essentials of a Good Research Design

The above definitions give the essentials of a good research design. They are:

1. It is a plan that specifies the objectives of the study and the hypotheses to be tested.
2. It is an outline that specifies the sources and types of information relevant to the research questions.

3. It is a blue print specifying the methods to be adopted for gathering and analyzing the data.
4. It is a scheme defining "the domain of generalizability, i.e., whether the obtained information can be generalized to a larger population or to different situations.

Nature of Research Design

A research design is indispensable for a research project. However, it is not a precise and specific plan like a building plan to be followed without deviations, but rather a series of guideposts to keep one going in the right direction. It is a tentative plan which undergoes modification, as circumstances demand, when the study progresses, new aspects, new conditions and new relationships come to light and insight into the study deepens. For example, the scope of a study may be narrowed down, when it is discovered that certain kinds of data are not available; the sampling method may be modified from 'random sampling' if a list of units of study with particulars of size is not readily available; and so on.

Besides, a research study cannot be as extensive and intensive as the researcher may like it to be. It has to be geared to the availability of data and the cooperation of the informants. It has also to be kept within the manageable limits, i.e., with the researcher's mental ability to grasp the implications, his competence and the amount of time and other resources available for this purpose. Thus, a research design "represents a compromise dictated by many practical considerations."

Why to Prepare a Research Design

Preparing a Research Design is an important stage in the process of conducting a research. According to P.V. Young; "Research design is the logical and systematic planning and directing of a piece of research." Research design is nothing but a scheme of work to be undertaken by a researcher at various stages. Systematic work of research and methodical conducting of various operations could be facilitated by a research design. It acts as a guide to achieve the decided goal of a researcher step by step. As research is a serious job, each piece of study is to be done calculative and cautiously. Completing the study within a prescribed time limit is another prerequisite of a research. The researcher must also complete his study within the specified cost. If the study is not completed within the specified period, it will increase the cost of research and may add to series of problems. Ultimately, the quality of the research will be affected. To avoid the discrepancies, proper planning of the research is essential and this is facilitated by a Research Design.

Initial Preparation

While preparing a Research Design, a researcher must give careful consideration to the following aspects:

1. The topic of the study must be chosen appropriately and the researcher must be thoroughly acquainted himself with the topic, issues and intricacies related to it.
2. It is also better for the researcher to verify other research designs prepared by different scholars.
3. As the cost and time are important aspects, the judgment and the rationality in deciding the above items must have the priority.
4. A design is susceptible to alterations. Hence, it is better to design it two or three times and perfect it after due consideration.
5. The researcher while pursuing various stages work must strictly follow the schedule mentioned in the design. Small modification without affecting the overall time schedule can be effected here and there.
6. As the sample is an important aspect of empirical research, once a method is decided, the researcher should stick on to it throughout the research.

When the study is completed and the report is ready, the original design can be modified in the light of the analysis of data and writing of the report. But care should be taken to avoid reshaping the original design. It may amount to distortion of the various process of the research study.

Body of a Research Design

A Research Design must contain the following aspects:

1. Introduction
2. Statement of the problem
3. Reference to previous studies made
4. Objectives of the study
5. Definition of concepts
6. Hypothesis
7. Limitations of the study
8. Methodology and techniques used in the study
9. Budget
10. Chapter Scheme.

1. Introduction

In the introduction, the researcher has to introduce the subject and relevant information relating to the topic of research. The researcher can quote authentic research studies and authors to support his views. Introduction should not be too lengthy. Over enthusiastic young researchers write long introduction running into number of pages like theory chapter. This is unwanted and may not fit in the pattern of crisp research design. As the purpose of introduction is to introduce the subject it is in the fitness of things be brief. Statistical information if at all needed and found relevant can also find a place in the introduction.

2. Statement of the Problem

The problem that has been chosen for research may have many facets. A problem can be analyzed from various angles. The focus of attention of the researcher towards the problem chosen must be pinpointed. The researcher must also point out the reason or reasons for choosing this particular problem for the research study. Hence, a researcher must analyze the following aspects in the statement of the problem:

(i) The need to study the problem of research.
(ii) What connotation does the problem contain?
(iii) Why this particular topic has been chosen by the researcher? Or what type of interest has evinced the researcher to undertake this study?

3. Reference of Previous Studies

Various research institutions and researchers bringing out research studies on similar topics. Referring such studies may be useful in many ways. It can impress upon the readers that the researcher has gone through the related studies. It can also help the researcher to locate a course of action for his study based on the earlier studies. It is enough if the important features of the studies and main findings are mentioned. Here also, researchers may be tempted to reproduce the original studies. This must be avoided. If possible, the researcher can give his own opinion about the previous studies. He can also explain the way in which he is going to improve his work upon the earlier studies. If new studies are made and if material is not available the researcher need not ponder over the previous studies, only research studies must be mentioned. In very many occasions we come across researchers referring to books and journals in the introduction which could be conveniently listed under bibliography section.

4. Objectives of the Study

While framing the objectives, it is better to limit the number of objectives to suit the needs of the topic. Framing of two many objectives may lead to confusion and the researcher may not be able to justify all of them.

The objective must be framed bearing in mind the topic of research. In other words, the objectives must elaborate the title and must indicate in its wordings the things to be investigated further. The objectives must also help to decide the chapters and analysis of various issues in each chapter. In other words, there must be a close and intimate relationship between the topic of research, objectives framed, chapter scheme and analysis of research. Objectives are also important to choose the relevant methods of research and tools to be followed. Framing of clear objectives can help the preparation of schedules immensely.

Languages and the contents of the objectives are as important as deciding the topic of research. The language jugglery must be clear, precise and meaningful. It must do away with playing of words. The contents must be expressed within a sentence.

5. *Definition of Concepts*

The important concepts that appear frequently in the study must be explained. These concepts, may relate to the title of research or the objectives or with the analysis. If suitable and authentic definitions are not found, the researcher can give his own working definition.

6. *Hypothesis*

A researcher can include hypothesis in the study or he can omit hypothesis. The need or otherwise of having hypothesis in a research study is a subject of controversy. The researcher has to make his own judgment, based on the nature of the study about the desirability of the inclusion of hypothesis. But once hypothesis is included, it must be tested. Through this test, it can be proved or disproved. A different style of language must be used to frame hypothesis. Degrees of comparison are to be necessarily used. The objectives of the study will provide guideline for framing the hypothesis.

7. *Limitations of the Study*

A study as well as the researcher is subject to limitations of time, cost, sample etc. While interviewing respondents, he has to face many difficulties. Eliciting of response may be difficult. The researcher can point out such limitations in his report.

8. *Methodology and Sampling*

Under this heading the researcher has to state the method

of research followed for his study and the tools and techniques of research used to collect data. The number of schedules prepared and the way in which data have been collected could also be explained.

The method of sample that has been followed for the study at various stages must also be mentioned. The researcher can give the sampling frame mentioning how he has arrived at the number of samples at various stages.

9. Budget

Though budget does not have a place in all research designs it must find a place in Research Projects aided by various sponsoring agencies. Time budget as well as cost budget must find separate place in the budget. The budget aids the researcher to complete the project within the stipulated cost.

10. Chapter Scheme

Last item of the Research Design is the Chapter Scheme. The number of chapters that the study contains and name of each chapter must be mentioned. The basis for the chapter scheme must include main findings prominently in independent chapters. The last chapter must always be the findings, conclusions and suggestions.

We have discussed the various components of research design. If scrupulously adhered to, these steps will ensure the success of a research project. The researcher design will also enable the optimum utilization of the time, energy, and sources at the disposal of the researcher. The scheduling of various steps and procedures are, nevertheless, tentative. A pragmatic research design can never be too rigid, and there must be provisions for small alternations based on the needs and circumstances.

23

Analysis of Data

Analysis and interpretation of data are the most crucial aspects of research. It is considered to be highly skilled and technical job, which should be carried out only by the researcher himself or under his close supervision. The analysis of data requires on the part of the researcher a thorough knowledge about the data, judgment skill, ability of generalization and familiarity with the background, objects and hypothesis of the study.

It is through a systematic analysis that the underlying features of the data are revealed and valid generalizations are arrived at. Facts and figures never speak for themselves. Organized data are more revealing than the facts figures. Only by means of organizing, analyzing and interpreting the research data their salient features, inter-relationship and cause and connections are brought out. The trends and sequences are elicited by means of generalizations. *Jules Henry Poincere* (Some Guiding Considerations in the Analysis of Research Data) says:

"The function of systematic analysis is to build an intellectual edifice in which properly sorted and gifted facts and figures are placed in their appropriate settings and consistent relationship so that general reference can be drawn from them the aim of the nature science."

According to Leon Festinger and Daniel Katz, the purpose of scientific analysis and interpretation of data are: *(i)* it should be productive *(ii)* be readily disposed to quantitive treatment *(iii)* have significance for systematic theory and *(iv)* can serve as a basis for broader generalization beyond the immediate content of the facts under study"
Steps in Analysis

While analyzing the research data the analyst is engaged in a series of routine procedures which have to be undertaken in a sequential manner. According to *Herbert Ayman* following are the steps in the analysis:

1. The data corresponding to each aspect of the phenomenon that have been conceptualized are tabulated for the aggregate group and provide a general statistical or quantitative description.
2. The data are similarly tabulated for each sub-group i.e., regarded as significant and provide the differentiated quantitive description desired as well as descriptions for any redefined population i.e., regarded as especially relevant to the problem.
3. Various modes of consolidating data for the many separate aspects of the phenomenon are employed to provide statistical description.
4. All this data are then examined in the context of related phenomenon so as to improve the evaluation of the finding.
5. A variety of qualitative non-statistical measures are used to supplement the quantitative description.

Statistical Tools

Statistics is an efficient tool in the analysis of research data. The very purpose of statistics is to aid research. According to *Mood:* "The statistician is engaged in producing tools for research workers." *E.G. Chambers* describes the utility of statistical methods as follows:

Statistical methods are to worker what tools are to the carpenter. The utility of statistics as a tool depends on the knowledge of their use for correct function. The craftsmen will not for instance use a mallet and chisel or a fresaw to plane a plank of wood, nor will he use a hammer to drive in a screw, similarly statistical tool must be only used for the specific purposes for which they have been devised.

A basic knowledge about statistics becomes inevitable for research workers, for systematic analysis and accurate and precise interpretation of data. Therefore understanding specific purposes for which different statistical tools are used as if methods of interpretation are a valuable asset to the researcher. Analysis of social data may be broadly classified into four broad categories, they are:

1. Methods which aim at summarizing the data and presenting the collective characteristics.
2. Methods used for comparison of two sets of data and assessing their difference.
3. Methods employed to assess the relationship between two or more variables.
4. Methods of prediction and forecasting.

The methods of analysis chosen for a particular study depends upon the nature of objectives, hypothesis to be tested and the purpose and use of the study. The commonly used statistical devices in social survey research are discussed in the following paragraphs.

1. Summarizing the data

Summarizing the data aims at presenting the collective characteristics of a given body of data. In summarizing the observations we first divide them on the basis of the different characteristics which normally fall in three classes viz., *(i)* normal characteristics or attributes, *(ii)* ordinal characteristics/qualitative variables, and *(iii)* interval variable/quantitative variables. The statistical methods used for assessing the collective characteristics are called the descriptive statistics. Descriptive statistics is concerned with summarizing the information that we have about characteristic no matter how may characteristics there are.

Normally such analysis relates to a single characteristic such as production, prices, sales etc. Such variables may either be a continuous one or a discrete one. A continuous variable has no break between one value and another (examples: age, weight, temperature etc.); whereas the discrete variables are a series of discontinuous variable without any continuity (example people, houses, automobiles). In other words those variables which cannot be broken into fractional units are discrete variables. Both theses types of variables may be compressed into statistical tables and analyzed for knowing the typical traits and features of such variables. This is known as summarization. There are two distinct sets of statistical processes used for summarization. They are: *(a)* Measures of Central Tendency and *(b)* Measures of Deviation of Dispersion.

A. Measures of Central Tendency

A set of statistical indexes are applied to find out the central tendency of the distribution. They are concerned as to how scores tend to cluster in a distribution. The commonly used measures of central tendency are; Mean, Median and Mode. Mean refers to the average value of the distribution which is arrived at by dividing the sum of scores in the distribution by number of observations.

Median is the mid-point of the array of scores. It is that value or point which divides the distribution equally. The scores are arranged in order of magnitude; and the middle point above and below which equal number of scores fall, is regarded as the median. In the case of grouped data the median position is located by means of identifying the class interval within which the middle value falls and then estimating the value of median. This method is called interpretation. Mode is that score which most frequently occurs in a distribution. Normally, mode can be located by means of inspection, in simple series. In a frequency distribution the mode is that point on the scale of variable where the frequency is the greatest.

Advantages of Measures of Central Tendency

- The measures of central tendency reduce the common characteristics of a given data into a simple representative number.
- The center of concentration of the scored and the most typically occurring scores are identified by means of these measures.
- They enable us to derive some meaning from the otherwise disorganized data, which is the basis for generalization.
- Measures of central tendency of a distribution help to forecast, estimate or determine the value that may occur in a given situation.

B. Measures of Dispersion

The purpose of the measures of dispersion or deviation is to describe how the scores are scattered or dispersed across the scale. Dispersion exists when the individual values of the observations are not identical to the mean value. The extent of dispersion, then, can be visualized as the extent to which the observation deviates from the mean. Some distributions may have the same average but greatly differ in their variability. In such a situation, the measures of dispersion will better represent the characteristics of the distribution that measures the central tendency. The Range, Mean Deviation, Standard Deviation and Quartile Deviation are the most common measures of dispersion.

Range

Range is the difference between the highest score and the lowest scores in a distribution i.e., Range is H-L. This is simple to calculate. Since it is based on only two values, it may not present a true picture of the characteristics of data. Extreme cases in either side may alter the value considerably.

Mean Deviation

It is statistical device intended to measure the extent of deviation of individual scores from the mean. The mean deviation or the average deviation is defined as the mean of the deviations of the individual scores from some measure of central tendency. It is arrived at by summing up the deviations irrespective of signs and dividing it by the number of observations.

Standard Deviation

The measures of variability are widely used. It is the square root of the sum of squared deviation divided by the number of observations. It is the standard measure of viability in most statistical procedures. A modified formula is used for calculating the Standard Deviation in a grouped data.

Quartile Deviation

It is also known as Semi-Inter-quartile Range. The distribution is divided into four equal parts. It is defined as the average amount by which the quartile point Q1 and Q3 deviate from the mean. Q1 is the point below which 25 percent of the scores fall and Q3 is the median which divides the scores equally.

2. Comparison and Assessing the Differences

Comparison of a bi-variate distribution and assessing the difference in two sets of observation is a common method of analysis in research. Generally a bi-variate table represents a joint distribution of two variables and a list of categories in each variable. A bi-variate distribution arises in either of two circumstances; Firstly, two characteristics of the same population say age and sex or income and employment are represented in a single table, one variable in the row and another in the column. This helps to assess the joint occurrence of the two characteristics. In the second category of bi-variate table, the universe, is divided into two categories of characteristics that must be present in every member of that category which is referred to as constant or condition. For instance the universe is divided into two parts on the basic geographic region and within each such region there are different characteristics such as income or education which are present in both population and are comparable. The comparative analyses of two sets of data are made by means of the following tools:

(i) Ratio

It is a common method of comparing frequencies. It is "merely an indicated or actual quotient which relates the size of one number to another". If there are two sets of figures to be compared, usually the figure in the right hand side of a distribution is reduced to 1 and thus allowing comparison to be made easy.

(ii) Proportion

"This measure is a fraction such that the numerator is one of two observed frequencies and the denominator the sum of observed frequencies." Proportion of two observations will be expressed in fraction of 1 and the total is always 1.

(iii) Percent

A proportion multiplied by 100 is called a percent. While reporting percentages, original frequencies must also be represented.

(iv) Rate of Change

It aims at comparing number with the number of potential events, i.e., number of individuals exposed to the risk of events. The comparison is accomplished by dividing the number of occurrences by the number of individuals exposed. This fraction is called the rate of occurrence.

(v) Percentage Change

The change that had taken place over a given period between the beginning year and terminal year is expressed in terms of percentage. The actual change is divided by original frequency and it is multiplied by 100, to arrive at the percentage change.

The purpose of using the above methods of comparison is to simplify the problem of comparison. They all serve to put qualitative characteristics into quantitative form. We are able to condense the information by the process of division. The basic difference in all these methods primarily lies in the method of selection of the base or denominator.

Testing the Difference between Two Groups

Testing the significance of the difference becomes a useful statistical method. It helps to solve an important and frequently occurring problem namely, whether there is real difference between two observational means or not? This type of analysis is highly useful in impact studies, hypothesis testing and in experimental researches. Both in experimentation and testing it serves as a useful tool. One fundamental difference between and testing is in experimentation we keep our subject constant and vary the subjects. In other words in experimentation we give our initial and final tests to the same group of objects by introducing the experimental factors. In the testing, on the other hand the conditions are kept constant and the standard measuring stick is used for variety of subjects. If conditions are not kept constant we may not be sure that changes observed between the two groups is due to the factor under study or due to other factors. Since experimentation is a remote possibility in social science research, the testing of different groups under identical condition is an accepted method of studying effect or impact of certain factors. In order to ascertain whether the difference observed between two groups or two experiments are significant or not, the following statistical tools are used.

1. Testing the Difference between two Means

By obtaining the mean and standard deviation of the groups, we can calculate't' statistics. It is essentially the ratio of the mean to its standard error; or it may be the ratio of a difference between means to its standard error."

It is a most important statistical tool; as such test is crucial in most researches. There are several methods of testing the difference between two means. The test may be for a single group tested before and after the introduction of an experimental factor or when two groups have been carefully equated for comparison. The four types of 't' test which are commonly used are: *(a)* test for large uncorrelated samples *(b)* test for large correlated samples, *(c)* test for small uncorrelated sample, and as *(d)* test for small correlated sample.

2. Significance of the Difference between two Percentages

Sometimes it happens that it is not possible to measure the presence or absence of quality but we know the percentage of those who possess a particular attribute. Testing the significance of the differences in two percentages will help to examine whether the proportion of one group possessing the same quality. This test is also based on the calculation of possessing the same quality. This test is also based on the calculation of standard error of difference between two percentages and the calculation of 't' on that basis. A different formulae is applied for this test.

Analysis of Variance

The 't' test is a statistical method used for testing. The significance of the difference lies between two groups or two sets of observation. When the groups to be compared are more than two, a different analysis is used for such comparison. The analysis of variance is a test of variability of a set of data. In any experiment, several factors may be at work which may result in the variability of the observations. The causes for such variability are isolated and their contribution on the variability is measured by means of this analysis, we may be able to ascertain whether the different groups represent a homogeneous population or are drawn from the heterogeneous population.

While grouping the observations into several independent classifications, it is seen that the classification is made on the basis of the characteristics we want to isolate as a causative factor for the variability. For example, if we want to analyze the variability of the loans obtained by farmers belonging to different size of holdings, from institutional agencies, we have to necessarily base the classification, on the farm size.

In order to determine the variability, within group variability and between group variability, have to be calculated. If they are approximately equal then it can be concluded that the groups are homogeneous. The more value of between groups exceeds that of 'within group' variance, the greater is the probability that the groups represent a different population. Thus,

Variance between groups

F =

Variance within Groups

The test of analysis of variance is based on the following three assumptions:

1. that the data are normally distributed
2. that the separate estimates are independent
3. that the variance in each class is the same.

Multiple Factor Analysis of Variance

In the single factor analysis of variance, the variability of a single independent variable is tested, whereas in multiple factor analysis, the variability of more than one independent variables at different levels are tested. Thus, multiple factor analysis of variance provides methods for testing. Whether different sub-groups or various combinations of sub-groups, represent different populations in terms of what is being measured as the dependent variable. For example the variances in I.Q. of the children of a particular class belonging to three different schools are measured. It is a simple analysis of variance involving only one factor. If a second factor, say, sex is introduced and further classification is made on that basis, there arises the multiple factor analyses of variance. Similarly, a third factor say, family background/ social status may be introduced. Thus, the different causes for the variability in the dependent factor namely I.Q. is brought out by means of this analysis.

3. *Test of Analysis*

Research is largely concerned with the identification of casual connections between different variables and studying the inter-relationship between them. The hypotheses framed by researchers are generally of statements of relationship between variables. Several techniques are used to test the extent of association between variables. Correlation is one such analysis which is more frequently used. When the two variables are numerical and normally distributed, the Product Moment Correlation analysis is the best. According to *Charmbers:* "This is by far the most useful and theoretically satisfactory method of measuring correlation and much advanced statistical work is based upon Product Moment Correlation." In this method, if the number of observations is within manageable limit, say 100 or 150 the data is grouped before calculation and a different procedure is applied.

When the actual value of two correlations cannot be accurately measured, and the distribution is not a normal distribution, we can rank the distribution and the correlation co-efficient is calculated on the basis using Spearman's Rank Order Correlation technique. Though this is an approximate estimate of correlation, it is simple to calculate. This correlation cannot be employed for further statistical analysis like partial and multiple correlation, factor analysis etc. In any correlation analysis a significant correlation co-efficient does not always prove a cause and effect relationship has to be supported by the researcher's interpretation, for a significantly high correlation may be due to either or all of the following reasons.

1. Cause and effect relationship between the two;
2. Both the variables may be influenced by a third variable; and
3. Co-variance may be accidental without any causative relationship.

When the test of association relates to some attributes or quantitative variables, the Chi square test of null hypothesis is used to determine the extent of association between variables.

Multi-Variable Relationship

It has been stated that one of the causes for the simple correlation may be the influences of a common variable. Such influences are not eliminated in the simple correlation analysis. In practical life situation problem, direct cause and effect relationship is a rare phenomenon to occur. Often times more than two variables are involved and any meaningful explanation for such phenomenon should take into account all those factors. Co-efficient of partial and multiple Correlations are the indexes used to measure the extent of correlation between two variables are kept constant; whereas the multiple correlations are the measurement of the combined effect of a group of independent variables on a dependent variable.

4. Prediction and Forecasting

Analysis of trend and forecasting the future is one of the purposes of research. Production and forecasting has greater relevance of disciplines like Economics, Commerce, Management and Cooperation. The basic requirement for the trend analysis and forecasting is the time series data for sufficiently long period. The prediction is a risk task and yet with the appropriate statistical device forecasting may be made with reasonable degree of accuracy. Here are some of the commonly used methods of trend analysis and forecasting.

Time Series Analysis

Time series is the data classified chronologically in terms of days, months or years, of a given variable. The fluctuation in the variable under study is due to the combined effect of four components viz., (1) secular trend (2) cyclical variation (3) seasonal variation and (4) irregular or random fluctuation. It is usually presented in the form of an equation.

O = T x C x S x I

The analysis of Time Series consists in separating these constituent parts by holding the other components constant. A measure of one of these components can be obtained by eliminating the remaining elements from the original data of the time series by the process of division. The model given above should be represented in percentages. If the absolute values are used the model is applied in the additive form i.e., O = T+C+S+I. Analysis of time series is useful in predicting the future tendencies. It is an essential aid in planning, allocation of resources and budgeting.

Measurement of Trend

The trend may be described in different methods. These methods aim at separating the trends by eliminating fluctuations. Prediction in such methods is made possible by means of extrapolation i.e., by projecting the trend line. It is possible by the following methods.

1. Curve by Inspection

It is the easiest method of all. The scribes is plotted on the graph and a smooth curve is drawn by inspection in such a way that the line lies between the points. The short term fluctuations are ignored; and it is seen that fluctuations are equal in both sides.

2. Semi Average Method

In this method the original series is divided into two equal parts, the value of each part is summed up and the average is arrived at separately. These two values are plotted on the graph at the central period of the part from which they have been calculated respectively. These are two values are then connected by a straight line.

3. Moving Average Method

It is another simple method in which the short term fluctuations are smoothened. The moving average may be calculated either for 3 years, 5 years, 7 years. The process of totaling and averaging starts in the middle year. For instance, if the average is for 5 years the averaging starts from 3rd year. The values of first two years of the first five year cumulative total is arrived at by adding 6th year value and deleting the value of the first year. This process is repeated for the whole series. To arrive at the average value, each year value is divided by a constant, the number of years for which moving average is calculated.

4. *Least Square*

If the data is linear the least square is an appropriate method. A graph of the series will be required to enable the decision to be made as to the curve to be fitted. The formula used is Y = a + bx; where y is the trend value or independent variable, 'a' is the constant, 'b' is the value determines the slope of the curve and 'x' denotes the year to which it pertains. It is most commonly employed and a satisfactory method.

5. *Regression*

Regression is an effective statistical tool to predict a bi-variate situation. It tells us the predicated value of a dependent variable 'x' and the constant 'a' and the regression co-efficient, 'b'. The formula used for linear regression is

Y = a + bx

This method is a logical extension of the correlation analysis, which implies co-variance. High correlation between 2 variables i.e., x and y will imply that predication is possible by means of regression analysis.

24

Editing, Coding and Tabulation of Research Data

Editing, coding and tabulation are the crucial stages in survey research It is at this the mass of data collected during the survey is processed with a view to reducing them to manageable proportions. Only by such a careful and systematic processing, the data will lend itself for statistical treatment and meaningful interpretation and conclusion. In other words the data processing which encompasses, editing, coding and tabulation, is an intermediary stage between the collection for data and their analysis and interpretation. Editing is a routine work: yet it has to be carried out with utmost care and devotion. Whereas coding in an operation which requires judgment skill, particularly for developing the coding frame. However, major part of the editing and coding involves repetitive and dull work of mechanical nature which, often times cause monotony and fatigue. Tabulation of data is a common tool in social sciences research used for summarizing the data so that they are amenable for interpretation. Thus, there are three important stages in the processing of social survey data.

They are:

1. Checking the filled questionnaire i.e., editing.
2. Reducing the mass of data into manageable proportion, i.e., coding.
3. Summarizing the data into tabular form.

Editing

Editing is the first and foremost stage in data processing. According to Pattern; "the process of examining the data collected in a survey to detect errors and omissions and to see that they are corrected and the schedules prepared for tabulation is known as editing." Editing involves routine task of checking the filled questionnaires. By means of careful editing, incorrect and incomplete answers are identified and inconsistencies are rectified. Once an error is left undetected at this stage it becomes rather impossible to rectify the mistake at subsequent stages; which goes unnoticed throughout the report. Editing thus becomes an absolute necessity for any large scale survey researcher, which uses questionnaire or interview schedules for the collection of research data. Moser emphasizes the need for coding thus;

"Before the questionnaires can be regarded as ready for coding, tabulation and analysis they should be checked for completeness, accuracy and uniformity."

In the process of editing the following points must be scrutinized:

1. Whether the data is reliable and accurate?
2. Whether the schedules are complete and whether all questions have been answered?
3. Whether the schedules are uniform?
4. Whether the entries have been made in accordance with the instructions?
5. Whether there are any inconsistencies in the answers?

The above questions are discussed elaborately in following paragraphs:

Completeness

At the editing stages it should be verified whether answers have been recorded for all the questions. Sometimes the investigators might have left the question inadvertently. Some questions, which are inapplicable, might have been skipped. The unknown and not applicable categories might have been left without any clear marking. Such gaps should be filled carefully at this stage. If there is any significant omission the reasons for such omissions should be found out. The possible reasons may be: *(a)* refusal to answer, *(b)* forgetfulness to record the information, and *(c)* not applicable. The not applicable cases should be recorded to avoid later confusion; the checking of incomplete answers of open ended question is more difficulty. The incomplete information can be gathered either with the information furnished by the interviewer himself of by approaching the respondent himself. Often times the information may be available in the schedules itself.

Accuracy

It is not enough that the information is complete; but its accuracy and truthfulness is more important. Clerical errors may arise due to carelessness in filling up the schedules. Sometimes the respondents may twist and distort the facts or provide faked information with a view to misleading the researcher or hiding some facts. The entries that are confusing and illegible have to be eliminated. In order to avoid inaccuracies and to ensure the reliability of information following steps should be taken:

1. The answers should as far as possible be pre-coded, as written answers are liable to more inaccurate.
2. Arithmetic such as totaling, subtracting etc., may be done leisurely in the office rather during the course of the interview
3. To ensure accuracy of certain key data, cross checking should be done by means of evolving different questions to elicit the same data information.

Uniformity

The purpose of editing is to convert the answers into uniform units of measurement before coding.

Its is a pre-requisite for accuracy, besides, editing ensures uniform interpretation of questions. At this stage questions are standardized; and the diverse answers will be transformed into uniform, comparable and homogeneous categories. For instance, while entering yearly income, some might have by mistake entered monthly income which has to be converted in to uniform pattern which will facilitate their further treatment, analysis and interpretation.

Consistency

Editing is a means for ensuring consistency of the data collected, and avoiding contradictions. The inconsistencies in the answers, if any have to be reconciled. For instance, the answers regarding the income of the respondents and the sale proceeds minus the cost of production must normally tally. If not, the inconsistencies and internal disparities may be corrected by examination and comparison of related replies.

At the editing stage, certain issues should be clarified so that the operation is completed with efficiency. They are discussed below.

Firstly, it is a common doubt whether the editing work is taken up for each question or for each section or for the complete questionnaire. It is always considered advantageous to edit the whole questionnaire, so that the logical link between various questions are understood and appreciated. Besides, this enables the cross checking of facts and information for ensuring their accuracy.

The second issue raised is whether all or only a sample of questionnaires need to be edited? There is no general rule as to this question

In any large-scale survey, thorough and complete editing scrupulously done would pay handsomely.

Thirdly, whether the editing should be done immediately or after the completion of the entire survey? In large scale surveys editing is done simultaneously by group leaders i.e., field editor while accepting the completed schedules form the investigators i.e., intake edit. It is always considered advantageous to complete the editing work simultaneously. This would enable the researcher to substantiate and complete the missing information from the fresh memories of the interview situation.

Coding

Coding is considered as the classification process. The purpose of coding is to classify the answers to a question into meaningful categories which in necessary for tabulation. In other words coding aims at summarizing the survey answers, so that the handling of such data is made easy for further analysis; and their essential pattern is brought out. Besides, coding is a useful means of quantifying the qualitative data. According to *Larton:* "coding consists in assigning a number of symbols to each answer which falls in a pre-determined class." *Goode and Hatt* define coding as follows:

"Coding is an operation by which data are organized into classes and number or symbol is given to each item according to the class in which it falls." Coding thus involves two important operation viz., *(i)* deciding the categories to be used, and *(ii)* allocating individual answers to them.

The desirability and profitability of coding however depends on the following factors.

1. The number of respondents
2. The number of questions asked and
3. The type of statistical operations planned

The need for coding arises more in the case of qualitative data which is not amenable for pre-coding and structuring of the interview schedule. Besides coding is a mean of quantifying the qualitative data which is a pre-requisite for any meaningful interpretation of social data. The method of coding also varies between the manual and machine processing of data. For manual tabulation any symbol is sufficient: whereas for machine tabulation it must be a numerical symbol. Furthermore, the number of classes is limited to 10 in the case of punch cards.

The task of coding may be dispensed with or substantially reduced if questions are pre-coded. By administering pre-coded questions time and money could be saved, and error in coding and transcriptions may be reduced considerably. One great hurdle in pre-coding is that it is not always possible to foresee the type of replies and answers of the respondents and as a result the classification becomes unrealistic. The answers tend to concentrate in the miscellaneous categories. However, pre-coding is highly useful for mechanical tabulation of data. The widely prevalent practice is to take up coding operation after completion of the collection of data.

Use of Coding

1. The difficult task of processing the qualitative information is made easy by means of coding. It serves as a useful method of utilizing the important sources of data, which cannot be pre-planned or patterned by narrow sets of questions such as historical records, case record, diaries, letters etc.
2. Coding is useful in structuring the questions after preparing the questionnaires/schedules which are done with unstructured questionnaires/schedules.
3. Only by careful coding umpteen variety of answers to open ended questions are reduced to manageable proportions. For example a question like; "What will you do with your increased income? May generate variety of response. The categorizing and grouping of answers provide a rational basis for classification of data and assigning codes.

Steps in Codes

1. *Study the Answers*

Before, commencing the coding operation, it is essential to clarify the meaning and purpose of the question. Unless we are clear in our minds as to what for the question is being asked, we cannot understand the answer in its proper perspective. The answer should be complete and clear. In case of any ambiguity, it should be developed in such a way as to reflect the intention of the respondents truly. The study of the answer is thus, the first stage in coding. In case of pre-coded questions, coding begins at the preparation of interview schedules.

2. *Preparation of Coding Frame*

Coding frame is developed by listing the possible answers to each question and assigning code numbers or symbols to each of them which are the indicators used for coding. Such indicators are developed gradually by classifying and grouping of survey data. While developing the coding frames it is always better to retain more number of groups so that it may be easy to amalgamate them later, if necessary, rather than to split to large groups. Such coding frame serves as the basis of coding the diverse answers which will not fall into neatly pre-arranged classes. Besides assigning code numbers or symbols to each group or category of answers, coding includes the preparation of a set of instructions which enable others to classify the comments and answers. The efficiency of coding largely depends on the soundness of the frame. As stated by Moser; "if it is not well constructed the order will come up against answers which either do not fit anywhere or might fit into several categories".

3. *Fit the Classes to the Data*

After preparing the sample frame the gradual process of fitting the answers to the questions must begin. The answers must be carefully studied, assigning the codes to them. The researcher has to use his common sense and discretion while assigning codes to the answers which are vague, deviant and difficult to understand. The answers which fall under unclassified categories may be treated as miscellaneous or residual category. The researcher should see that no answer is left uncoded, by proper checking.

4. *Transcription*

Transcription means transferring of the information from the schedules to a separate sheet called transcription sheet. Transcription sheet is a large summary sheet which contains the answers/code of all respondents. It is useful to have an overview of all the illustrations of all respondents. Preparation of tables becomes easy by means of consolidation, grouping and classification of data. It also enables the comparison of variables and preparation of cross tables. Transcription is a time-saving and error preventing device which renders efficient management of data. Transcription may not be necessary when only simply tables are required and the number of respondents is few.

Principles in Designing Codes

Milred Parten has laid down certain principles in designing codes they are:

1. The classification should be detailed as combining is relatively simple.
2. Codes need not always be in numerical form unless mechanical tabulation is needed
3. For mechanical tabulation, the codes must be numerical and the classes should be limited to10.
4. Items which are pre-coded be prepared to ensure uniform coding.
5. Code instructions should be prepared to ensure uniform coding.
6. Classification must follow certain standards and similar to those used in other studies which will be useful in interpretation of results or for comparison.
7. Class intervals should be clear and specific without overlaps.

8. Accuracy and completeness should be checked after coding.
9. Arithmetic computations should be complete before commencing the coding operations

Problems in Coding

The Common problems encountered by the researcher/ coder while coding are as follows:

1. When the matter to be coded involves certain concepts which are not understood by the respondents in the same sense, the answers will also be diverse and unrelated to the concept. This defect is difficult to rectify at the coding stage.
2. Sometimes the researcher/interviewer fails to elicit the desired data, which is revealed only at the time of coding.
3. Sometimes it is discovered to the dismay of the researcher that the answers to questions are not of uniform type, which defeats the purpose of coding.

Tabulation

Tabulation is a means for proper interpretation of the research data. The tabulation is a procedure which involves arranging of assembled data in a logical, concise and systematic manner on the basis of the following criteria: *(i)* geographical, *(ii)* chronological or temporal, *(iii)* qualitative or attributive *(iv)* quantitative. On the Basis of the above classifications, the number of cases following in each class is counted and is sorted into relevant classes.

The following principles have to be observed generally while preparing the tables.

1. The pattern of classification is made on the basis of the purpose and objectives of the study and problem in hand.
2. The tables are prepared with reference to the hypothesis, which have a direct bearing on the method of analysis.

3. The tables should properly represent the data collected and their basic features.

Frequency Distribution

It is the simplest form of tabulation. There will be two columns in the frequency tables. In one column the different qualities of an attribute and different values are entered in the second column. Following are the important considerations in preparing the frequency tables:

(a) Values are entered in the left hand column and the frequencies are entered in the right hand column.

(b) The value or classes should be mutually exclusive; overlapping values will only lead to confusion.

(c) The ordering of data should be logical.

(d) The class intervals should be carefully chosen, ordinarily there should not be less than 8 or 10 classes and more than 20 classes.

(e) The class intervals should be neither too big nor too small, as very small ones becomes irrelevant and very big ones tend to conceal the important characteristics.

(f) They should be of convenient number of 5 or 10 instead of 7 or 9. Definite lower and upper limits should be clearly designated so as to avoid any confusion.

Mechanical Tabulation

Tabulation may be done either manually or mechanically. For mechanical tabulation the coded answers have to be transferred to the punch cards. Separate card normally contains 80 columns and the code number of each answer is punched by hand operated punching machine. Punching so done is verified by another machine which assures the accuracy of punching. If there is any discrimination, such cards are verified and in case of mistakes they are replaced. Subsequently these cards are fed to sorting machine which sort the cards into the number of categories punched in the cards for each question. The sample frequency tables and complicated cross tables are carried in sort time with precision and efficiency. However the need for mechanical tabulation hardly arises in surveys involving small size samples and simple analysis. Following are the circumstances in which the mechanical tabulation is advisable.

a. If the survey involves large number of samples, tabulation by machine is useful and economical.

b. If the study aims at complicated cross tabulation and advanced analysis, mechanical tabulation will ensure more accuracy.

c. Machine tabulation provides lot of flexibility to the researcher. Tabulation can be done within no time as little effort is involved. It gives incentive and scope to try new patterns and methods of analysis.

Disadvantages

Mechanical tabulation should not be considered as unmixed blessing. The desirability or resorting to mechanical device is deterred for two important considerations.

a. The machine tabulation is a costly affair and therefore is out of reach for many researchers. Its prohibitory cost renders this method unsuited to the low budget researchers.

b. The machine tabulation requires expert advise.

c. The researcher has to depend on others for punching, sorting and tabulation, unlike hand tabulation which may be done by the researcher himself.

Thus, neither the advantages nor the disadvantages can be categorically stated. As stated by Moser; "For any survey which involves large number or for which a larger number of cross-tabulations are required machine method has much to commend them. These cases apart, hand tabulation have much in its favour." The nature of the survey and the needs and requirements of the analysis are the chief factors which determine the need or otherwise of mechanical devices in preparation of tables.

25

Research Report Writing

Report writing is the culmination of any research investigation as the research worker is obligated to report his study on its completion. Only at this stage the researcher assembles the findings of the study, draws conclusions and evaluates his own findings. By means of the research report the researcher is able to communicate to the readers his findings and conclusions in a form which is readily understood and assessed, as also the validity verified by the evidence produced in support of the conclusions. Reporting is thus the end product of a research activity. It is a highly skilled work, which is both interesting as well as challenging. Report writing is a technical activity which "requires considerable thought" effort, patience, skill and penetration and an overall approach to the problem data, and analysis as well as firm control over language and greater objectivity. Considerable amount of planning and preparation is necessary for organizing and writing the report. Besides, perfection in the research report is achieved by continuous and perfection in thought and creative and intelligent writing. It is a time consuming process, and normally about 25 to 30% of the budget time of a research should be earmarked for writing the reports.

Before actually planning for writing the report, the

researcher should clarify certain issues.

Firstly, the researcher should be clear about the point whether the report is meant for publication? Who will undertake the publication? Who will meet the cost? Whether the agency sponsoring the research is interested in publishing the report?

Secondly, the researcher should have a prior knowledge about the process of reproduction of the research report that is whether the report is to be typed? Mimeographed? Printed? Or photo lithographed? This will enable the researcher to adapt his plan accordingly, as each method has certain do's and don'ts. For instance in photolithograph, last minute changes cannot be made as on other methods of duplication. Generally the method of reproduction depends on: *(a)* size of report, *(b)* type of readers, *(c)* number of copies likely to sell, *(d)* the desired format, and *(e)* financial budget etc.

Thirdly, the researcher should be clear about the point who will read the report or of whom the report is meant? There are three broad categories of such readers: *(i)* the layman and the general public, *(ii)* the administrator and the project sponsor, and *(iii)* the fellow researcher and the technical expert.

Report for Layman

The preparation of research report for layman is a trying task. It must be interesting, simple and lucid. It must avoid all technical jargons and details as to the methods of investigation.

Report for the Administrator

Such reports should neither be too general nor too technical. It may contain some technical aspects, but on the whole simple and direct. The recommendations must be specific for the administrator to give effect to.

Technical Report

In such report the researcher is expected to give a full

account of the technical aspects both in the sampling methods and subject matter. Fellow professionals are more concerned about the methods, as they want to know the accuracy of the investigation. Conceptual and analytical frame work and sample design should be adequately explained. *M.H. Gopal* points out four distinguishing facts of technical report.

1. The problem and its nature.
2. The method and its scientific accuracy.
3. The data and their dependability.
4. The logical relationship of the data and the interpretation.

These facts have to be presented logically and sequentially with simplicity, clarity and brevity. The research report is not usually presented to the popular lay audience, since this task is taken over by the journalists.

Planning and Organizing the Report

Before starting the report writing a good deal of planning is necessary. Planning and organizing the study materials form the basis of organizing the research report. While commencing the report writing, the researcher, particularly the beginners do not know how to start writing. Researcher would have at this stage accumulated volley of data and information which have to be prudently used in the study. The author's mind is crowded with ideas and a jumble of thoughts. A well conceived planning and organizing the report facilitates report writing with proper emphasis to different aspects. Planning permeates the entire report-to each chapter, aspects and paragraph. It is nothing but arrangement of ideas in a logical and coherent manner within the frame work of the overall structure laid down. Following are the advantages of planning and organization of the report:

1. Ideas and facts which are relevant to the study alone are included in the report by screening them at the stage of planning.

2. The report gets greater clarity and unity.
3. Research findings and result can be easily communicated to the readers.
4. It facilitates the transition of ideas, ease in passing from one idea to another.
5. Planning ensures unity and sequence in presentation of facts i.e., one idea at a time, and a series of ideas one after another.
6. The planning results in an integrated and comprehensive research report.

Steps in Organization

Planning and organization of the research report involve the following three steps: (A) Organizing the research notes (B) Reflective thinking, and (C) Formation of an outline.

(A) Organizing the Research Notes

Notes taking are the core activity in social research. The process of notes taking starts even before the selection of research topic. Such notes are helpful in every stage of research from the selection of topic till the completion of the final report. The accuracy and utility of the notes taken from wide ranging literature as also from field observation had to be put to optimum use while writing the report. Methodical and systematic organizing of notes is a prerequisite for effective writing. Following points have to be adhered to while organizing research notes.

1. For taking down notes, it is always better to use cards rather than sheets of paper. Writing in sheets of paper may not ensure accuracy and adequate control over the facts and may lead to confusion.
2. The cards have to be assorted and arranged topically. Such arranging of notes and putting them under major heads is necessary before commencing the writing.
3. After organizing the notes under different heads

the researcher should review them, and consider their adequacy. If the researcher finds any notes being inadequate he has to gather additional information.

(B) Reflective Thinking

Research is a thinking process. It is not a mechanical work of gathering information and presenting them. Instead it is a lively, thrilling, soul satisfying experience. The thinking process starts even before choosing a research topic. Reasoning power of the researcher is the efficient tool for research decisions, interpretation and generalization and giving meaningful recommendation. Besides, defining and delimiting different concepts, choosing the right methodology and tool are all the result of deep, continuous and lively thinking. At the writing stage it is all the more necessary, as clear thinking alone results in clear writing. As Whitney puts it: "there is a highly positive correlation between good thinking and effective writing." The reasoning process helps to present a clear and straight forward exposition of the ideas.

According to *M.H. Gopal,* "Research is not merely the accumulation, evaluation and assimilation of facts; it is also and more so re-building them into meaningful whole. This demands patient, deep and alert thinking." The researcher must therefore develop his thinking faculty and train himself in the thinking process.

(C) Outlining

Drafting an outline is a natural sequence and an outcome of thinking. The outline of the research study is made at two stages. One, at the beginning of the study which serves as a design of the study and the second before writing the report. The outline prepared for the purpose of reports writing should be elaborate so as to include all important aspects which should find a place in the report. Such an elaborate report renders the drafting easy and gives direction to the writing. In the words of *Parten:* "Generally the report secures greater clarity and unity if the entire report is first outlined under large heading and then filled in by more and more detailed outline." To make the outline elaborate, it should be prepared at three stages; topical outline, paragraph outline and broad aspects outline. Topical outline includes the chapters and broad aspects to be included in each chapter. It is a skeleton outline. Paragraph outline includes all major paragraphs, indicating the central idea of each paragraph. It is merely composed of points to be included in sentences. *M.H. Gopal* suggests the following points to be observed while planning an outline.

1. It should be as detailed as possible and should enable continuous writing.
2. It should not be as vague, and should not include, such vague phrases as 'introduction 'body' conclusion etc, which give no direction to the report writing.
3. It should fulfill the considerations of chronology, topical unity, coherence and transition.
4. Each paragraph should contain one major idea.

The following outline may be adopted while preparing the research report.

Outline

I. Pre-factory Material

1. Title Page
2. Table of contents
3. List of illustrations, tables and charts
4. Preface or foreword.

II. Text or body of report

1. Introduction

(a) Objectives of the study, statement of the problem, definition of concept and hypotheses.

(b) Time, place and material of the survey,

(c) Scope, assumption and limitations,

(d) Organization and sampling procedures,

(e) Methods, tools and techniques employed for data collection.

2. *Analysis and Presentation of Results*

(a) Report of facts-nature, volume and dimension,

(b) Statistical analysis of data,

(c) Interpretation, generalization and conclusions,

(d) Summary of findings and recommendations.

III. Supplementary Material

1. Appendices – questionnaires, statistical tables, techniques
2. Bibliography
3. Index
4. Glossary of terms.

The title page contains the title of the report, name of the author, sponsoring organization, place and data of publication and publishers. The table of contents includes outline of the topic, headings and sub-headings. Some authors suggest the inclusion of summary of findings and recommendations in the prefatory material, but it is customary to present them at the end of the report.

Conclusion and Generalization

The primary task in social surveys is that the data presented in tabular from should first be discussed and explained. At the same time the researcher should avoid repeating the whole data that the table contains. One has to be selective in explaining the table. While explaining tables it is always necessary to cite relevant column numbers and row numbers for the convenience of the readers. The statistical materials presented in the tables should be systematically checked for accuracy. Besides explaining the tables, the researcher has to interpret the data on the basis of the evidences. Such interpretation is the basis of generalization. It should be honest and straight forward exercise. He should prefer understatement instead of overstatement in order to retain readers' confidence. While drawing conclusions he has to follow certain principles as laid down by Parten. Data should be scrutinized to see whether: *(i)* it is possible to come to opposite conclusions with the same material, *(ii)* other persons on the staff would reach the same conclusions with the evidence shown, *(iii)* conclusions are consistent with the one another and with other known facts, *(iv)* they seem to sense and if not why? *(v)* they are coloured by the writer's personal biases, *(vi)* their meaning is unmistakable, *(vii)* they could be accounted for by the survey techniques used.

Arrangement of Ideas

Arrangement of ideas and the methodical and or the systematic presentation is an aid to draw the attention and evoke the interest of the readers. According to *Carter V. Goode:* "the skilful writer leads his reader step by step through a well organized analysis of problem, method, data and conclusions." Headings should be specific, brief and represent the content. Such headings and sub-headings call the attention of readers as to the materials presented. In the opinion of Parten: "Logical relationship of various points can be brought out by organizing the points, by appropriately employing centre heading, sub-headings, under lining bold face type etc." Besides there must be uniformity and consistency in presentation of ideas. Punctuation, capitalization, abbreviations, footnotes, quotations, acknowledgement and bibliography must follow a uniform pattern. Frequent paragraphing, topical and summary sentences at the beginning and end of paragraphs, capitalization of key phrases and sentences will make the presentation meaningful and logical.

Writing Style

Utmost attention should be paid for writing the research report. The report is a communication process between the researcher and the reader. The report should be clear, easy to read and accurate in information and statements. Vagueness, generalization and presumptions will make the report incomplete and uninteresting. The essence of communication is clarity in presentation. According to M.H. Gopal the following factors influence good write-up: *(a)* the reader in view; *(b)* how technical the problem is; *(c)* the researcher's hold over his facts and techniques; *(d)* his command over language; and *(e)* the form and fullness of the notes i.e.., of the data and *(f)* documentation.

The first step in clear presentation is clear thinking. The poor writing is largely due to hazy thinking on the problem in question. Only by thinking the researcher develops originality, which is reflected in his report. Research report writing is a reasoning process and without clarity of thought there won't be clarity in writing.

Next the researcher should have a good command over the language. Often, a poor writing is the result of the researcher's inadequate command over language "Too frequently faulty sentence structure, illogical paragraphing, poor punctuation, incorrect spelling and other variations of English render an otherwise promising manuscript virtually worthless." At the same time the researcher should not use complex high sounding language at the cost of clarity and straight forward presentation. Researcher is often, tempted to write with an eye more towards style than clarity, drama than facts and persuasiveness than incisiveness." The researcher should always remember that he is writing a scientific report and not a magazine article.

Brevity is another point the researcher should keep in mind while writing his report. He should take care of the economy of words and concentration of ideas which will lead to density and poignancy. Repetition and superfluousness will obstruct the lucidity of the report and will interfere with precision and clarity.

Objectivity is yet another principle in report writing. The report writer should write an unbiased, objective report fortified by facts. It should convince the audience of the truth of the ideas present.

The research report normally goes through three drafts.

The objectives of the first are comprehensiveness and fullness of facts. The first draft should be written as rapidly as possible and without any break. An uninterrupted period is conducive for integrated presentation. In the subsequent drafts the report should be improved both in the form and the language, by considerable trimming, pruning and chiseling. Ideas and sentences have to be realigned by cutting and joining, so that the report gets clarity, order, logic, unity, coherence and naturalness.

Furthermore, the researcher in his draft should take care to avoid too much technical jargons, complex and mate languages and repetition. He should also avoid using words with the same meaning, unspecific and redundant words and personal references like "I" "We" etc.,

By patient review of the written materials, improving the draft and by giving more thought and effort, the write up could be made effective and poignant. Before giving final touch up to the report, it is better to keep the manuscript aside for a while so that it gets cold. The gaps and weakness come to limelight only after a lapse of time when the material is carefully re-examined and re-edited.

Graphic/Diagrammatic Presentation

Presentation of research data in the form of charts and diagrams is a method of attracting the attention of the readers. Besides, this enables the complex facts to be grasped more readily. Bar charts, component bar charts, pie diagram and pictogram are the methods more commonly used. Bar chart is useful in comparing two groups each having sub-strata which are components of the whole. Pie chart, like the component bar chart shows the relationship of parts to the whole. Pictogram has greater appeal and represents the data in small symbols or simplified pictures and is useful in visual comparison as in the case of bar chart. Besides the chart, the graph is also one of the most common devices for providing trend. The map is useful in ecological analysis to show the position of natural barriers or endowments, location of industries, flow of commerce and traffic etc.

Such aids, according to Goode and Hatt "not only present the data in readable form but also help the reader to understand the more complex tabulations." These are common aids to clarify and are explained in any book on business or research statistics.

Footnotes and Bibliography

Documentation is one of the important components of research report. Footnotes and bibliography are the reference to the sources from which ideas, data facts and opinions are borrowed from previous or current works. It makes the citations more authoritative, adds to the growth and continuity of knowledge and an acknowledgement of the benefits the researcher received from other's writings. Footnote serves the following specific purpose:

1. It gives credit to previous authors who have tackled the problem.
2. The larger context of the problem is indicated to the reader.
3. The researcher's contribution is distinguished from those of others.
4. The researcher is protected from being attacked by others.
5. It provides a reference to the sources which may be consulted for more details.

While citing references the researcher must keep in mind certain points. Well-known facts need not be cited. It is always better to cite scholarly editions than the ordinary sources. If the content of the citation has already appeared in the text, such citation should be avoided lest it results in repetition. Too lengthy and controversial quotations should be relegated to the appendix. The footnotes must be relevant and the researcher must avoid the tendency to overwhelm the reader with quotations. As M.H. Gopal puts it, over-documentation is bad, but under-documentation is worse. The citations should fit in with the text, relevant, clear and factual and sources must be cited fully and correctly.

Select Bibliography

1. Abrams, Mark, *Social Surveys and Social Action,* London: William Heinemann Ltd., 1951.
2. Anderson, R. and Zelditch Morris Jr. *A Basic Course in Statistics with Sociological Application,* New York: Holt, Rinehart and Winston Inc., 1975.
3. Best John, *Research in Education,* New Delhi: Prentice Hall of India Pvt. Ltd., 1963.
4. Blalock Jr. Herbert, M. and Blalock Ann, B. Methodology in Social Research New York: McGraw Hill Book Company, 1968.
5. Borg, Walter, R., *Educational Research: An Introduction,* New York; David Mckay Company, 1976.
6. Chou-Ya Lun, *Statistical Analysis,* New York: McGraw Hill Book Company, 1968.
7. Chambers, E.G. *Statistical Calculation for Beginners,* London: Cambridge University, 1955.
8. Cordasco Fransìsco and Gatner Elliot, *Research and Report Writing,* New York: The Dryden Press, 1953.
9. Festinger, Leon and Katz, Daniel, *Research Methods in Behavioural Sciences,* New York: The Dryden Press, 1953.
10. Goode and Scates, *Methods of Research,* New York: Appleton-Century Crofts, 1954.
11. Goode, Carter V., *Essentials of Educational Research,* New York: Appleton Century Crofts, 1966.

12. Goode, William J. and Hatt, Paul K., *Methods in Social Research*, London: McGraw Hill Book Company, 1964.
13. Gopal M.H., *An Introduction to Research Procedure in Social Sciences*, Mumbai, Asia Publication House, 1964.
14. Gopal, M.H., *Research Reporting in Social Science*, Dharwar: Karnatak University, 1965.
15. Hyman Herbert, *Survey Designs and Analysis*, Illinois: The Free Press Publishers, 1955.
16. Hillaway, Tyrus, *Introduction to Research*, Boston: Hougton Mifflin Co., 1965.
17. Macdougall, Curits D, *Interpretative Reporting*, New York: The Macmillan Company, 1961.
18. Moser, C.A., *Survey Methods in Social Investigation*, London: William Hienemann Ltd., 1959.
19. Murdick Robert, *G. Business Research – Concepts and Practice*, Florida, International Book Company. 1959.
20. Parten, Mildred, *Surveys, Polls and Sample; Practical Procedures*, New York: Harper and Row, John Weatherhill Inc, 1965.
21. Rummel, J.F. and Ballaine, W.C. *Research Methodology in Business*, New York: Harper and Row, 1963.
22. Selltiz Clarire, Jahoda Maria, et. al., *Research Methods in Social Relations*, USA: Methuen & Co., 1967.
23. Travers, Robert M.V., *Introduction to Educational Research*, New York: the Macmillan Co., 1958.
24. Whitney, F.L., *The Elements of Research*, New York: Asia Publishing House, 1961.
25. Young, P.V., *Scientific Social Surveys and Research*, New York: Asia Publishing House 1962.
26. Cordasco and Catner, *Research and Report Writing*, New York: Barnes Noble Inc., 1956.
27. Krishnasami, O.R., *Research Methodology in Social Sciences*, Himalaya Publishing House, Mumbai.

Model Questions

Short Questions

1. Give the definition of Research.
2. Examine the characteristics of Research.
3. Define 'concept' and 'theory'.
4. Explain the importance of hypothesis.
5. Discuss various types of hypothesis.
6. How to test a hypothesis?
7. Compare pure and applied research?
8. What is problem oriented research?
9. Explain the features and uses of feasibility research.
10. Discuss the steps involved in historical research.
11. Explain the steps in case study. What are its uses?
12. Discuss the features of survey?
13. What are the purposes of survey?
14. What is a research problem?
15. How will you identify a research problem?

16. Explain the need to review literature.
17. What are the forms of interaction?
18. Define a seminar and workshop.
19. Differentiate a schedule and a questionnaire.
20. Explain the questions to be avoided in a schedule.
21. What are the advantages of an interview?
22. What are the qualities of an interviewer?
23. Define observation. What are its contents?
24. Explain a scale.
25. Define sampling.
26. Define the features of random sampling.
27. What are the essentials of a research design?
28. Define mean and mode.
29. What is ANOVA?
30. What is time series analysis?
31. What is coding?
32. Explain various methods of coding.

Essay Questions

1. Define social research and explain its importance.
2. Explain the role of theory and hypothesis in social research.
3. Give an account of various methods of social research.
4. Explain the areas and types of evaluation studies.
5. Define action research.
6. What are the uses of historical research?
7. Define and explain the significance of case study.
8. Explain in brief the social survey.
9. What are the advantages of surveys?
10. What is experimental research?
11. Explain the sources of a research problem.

12. Explain the significance of research gap.
13. Discuss the need and mode of interaction with research experts.
14. What is the relevance of seminars to a researcher?
15. Explain the steps in preparing a schedule.
16. What are the limitations of a questionnaire? How will you overcome them?
17. Explain the steps involved in conducting an interview.
18. Discuss various forms of observation. What are its uses?
19. What are the uses of scales to social research?
20. Explain the uses of library in social research.
21. Discuss in brief various methods of sampling.
22. Explain the body of a research design.
23. Discuss in brief the importance of editing.
24. Explain the contents of a research report.